Artificial Intelligence Enters the Marketplace

Bantam Computer Books
Ask your bookseller for the books you have missed

THE AMIGADOS MANUAL
  by Commodore-Amiga, Inc.
THE APPLE //c BOOK
  by Bill O'Brien
ARTIFICIAL INTELLIGENCE ENTERS THE MARKETPLACE
  by Larry R. Harris and Dwight B. Davis
THE COMMODORE 64 SURVIVAL MANUAL
  by Winn L. Rosch
COMMODORE 128 PROGRAMMER'S REFERENCE GUIDE
  by Commodore Business Machines, Inc.
THE COMPUTER AND THE BRAIN
  by Scott Ladd / The Red Feather Press
EXPLORING ARTIFICIAL INTELLIGENCE ON YOUR APPLE II
  by Tim Hartnell
EXPLORING ARTIFICIAL INTELLIGENCE ON YOUR COMMODORE 64
  by Tim Hartnell
EXPLORING ARTIFICIAL INTELLIGENCE ON YOUR IBM PC
  by Tim Hartnell
EXPLORING THE UNIX ENVIRONMENT
  by The Waite Group / Irene Pasternack
FRAMEWORK FROM THE GROUND UP
  by The Waite Group / Cynthia Spoor and Robert Warren
HOW TO GET THE MOST OUT OF COMPUSERVE, 2d EDITION
  by Charles Bowen and David Peyton
HOW TO GET THE MOST OUT OF THE SOURCE
  by Charles Bowen and David Peyton
MACINTOSH C PRIMER PLUS
  by The Waite Group / Stephen W. Prata
THE MACINTOSH
  by Bill O'Brien
THE NEW *jr*: A GUIDE TO IBM'S PC*jr*
  by Winn L. Rosch
ORCHESTRATING SYMPHONY
  by The Waite Group / Dan Shafer with Mary Johnson
PC-DOS / MS-DOS
User's Guide to the Most Popular Operating System for Personal Computers
  by Alan M. Boyd
POWER PAINTING: COMPUTER GRAPHICS ON THE MACINTOSH
  by Verne Bauman and Ronald Kidd / illustrated by Gasper Vaccaro
SMARTER TELECOMMUNICATIONS
Hands-On Guide to On-Line Computer Services
  by Charles Bowen and Stewart Schneider
SWING WITH JAZZ: LOTUS JAZZ ON THE MACINTOSH
  by Datatech Publications Corporation / Michael McCarty
UNDERSTANDING EXPERT SYSTEMS
  by The Waite Group / Mike Van Horn
USER'S GUIDE TO THE AT&T PC 6300 PERSONAL COMPUTER
  by David B. Peatroy, Ricardo A. Anzaldua, H. A. Wohlwend, and Datatech
  Publications Corporation

Artificial Intelligence Enters the Marketplace

*Larry R. Harris
and Dwight B. Davis*

BANTAM BOOKS
TORONTO · NEW YORK · LONDON · SYDNEY · AUCKLAND

ARTIFICIAL INTELLIGENCE ENTERS THE MARKETPLACE
A Bantam Book / June 1986

Cover design by J. Caroff Associates.
Photograph of Dwight Davis courtesy of Cheryl M. Dunphy

ISBN 0-553-34293-2

Published simultaneously in the United States and Canada

PRINTED IN THE UNITED STATES OF AMERICA

FG   0 9 8 7 6 5 4 3 2 1

Contents

Preface   ix

1. AI Comes of Age   1
    THE MEANING OF INTELLIGENCE   4
    A WHIRLWIND EVOLUTION   6
    THE ROOTS OF AI   8
    A MARKET RIPE FOR AI   10
    COMPUTERS AS TOOLS   13

2. Foundations   15
    COMPUTER HIERARCHY   19
    PROGRAMMING LANGUAGES   23
    RULE-BASED PROGRAMMING   30
    LISP AND LISP MACHINES   34

3. Natural Language Processing   37
    NATURAL LANGUAGE HISTORY   41
    SYNTAX—RULES OF GRAMMAR   43
    SEMANTICS—SHADES OF MEANING   50
    PRAGMATICS—DETERMINING INTENT   52
    LEVEL OF SEMANTIC PRIMITIVES   53
    SOLVING THE ENTIRE PROBLEM   54
    CONCEPTUAL VIEW   55
    AMBIGUITY   57
    AGGREGATES   58

SUMMARIZATION   60

DATA ANALYSIS CAPABILITY   62

SPEECH   63

4. *Expert Systems*   65

DECISION TREES   69

KNOWLEDGE BASES   72

KNOWLEDGE BASE QUERY   76

SIMULATING HUMAN PROBLEM SOLVING   77

FROM INFERENCING TO INTELLIGENT BEHAVIOR   79

KNOWLEDGE-BASED SYSTEMS   80

CHOOSING THE PROBLEM   82

5. *AI Products Emerge*   85

INHERENT DIFFICULTIES   89

ACADEMIC MINDSET   90

TECHNOLOGY-DRIVEN VERSUS MARKET-DRIVEN PRODUCTS   92

EXPERT SYSTEM STATUS   93

CHOOSING A PRODUCT NICHE   95

CUSTOM DEVELOPMENT   96

KNOWLEDGE ENGINEERING TOOLS   98

VERTICAL APPLICATIONS   101

THE ROLE OF BUSINESS   102

SOCIETAL RESTRICTIONS   103

6. *Japan Inc.*   109

THE FIFTH GENERATION   112

PARALLEL-PROCESSING GOALS   114

KNOWLEDGE BASES   117

THE LISP VERSUS PROLOG DEBATE   117

REVOLUTIONARY OR EVOLUTIONARY?   120

A HISTORY OF SUCCESS   122

CAN INCOMPATIBILITY SUCCEED?   124

AN ACE IN THE HOLE   126

7. *Maintaining the U.S. Edge*   129
    THE GOVERNMENT'S ROLE   132
    A CONSORTIUM OF COMPETITORS   137
    HANDICAPPING MCC'S PROSPECTS   140
    THE ENTREPRENEURIAL LURE   142
    A RISKY BUSINESS   145
    EDUCATIONAL SHORTCOMINGS   149

8. *Near-Term AI*   153
    ILLEGITIMATE AI CLAIMS   156
    UNNEEDED AI PRODUCTS   158
    AI ON PERSONAL COMPUTERS   160
    THE NEXT FIVE YEARS   161
    BUILD YOUR OWN   163
    CONVERSING WITH COMPUTERS   165
    COMPUTER-ASSISTED INSTRUCTION   167
    SPEECH RECOGNITION AND VISION   169

9. *What the Future Holds*   173
    WILL MACHINES REALLY THINK?   176
    THE AI LANDSCAPE   177
    GENERATING NEW KNOWLEDGE   180
    MACHINES THAT LEARN   182
    KNOWLEDGE OF THE SELF   184
    THE CURIOSITY TO KNOW   185

Index   187

Preface

When I first contemplated writing a book about artificial intelligence, the field was just beginning to enter the commercial realm and the public's consciousness. Today artificial intelligence, or AI, has become one of the hottest topics of computer research. It has also been embraced by a wide variety of computer hardware and software vendors, who claim with varying degrees of justification to offer revolutionary products based on AI technology. Scarcely a week passes without some new company joining the AI multitude.

The past year's activity, however, hasn't necessarily served to remove people's uncertainty about what AI is or about what potential the field holds. In fact, exaggerated and conflicting vendor claims about products using AI techniques probably have resulted in increased confusion and skepticism.

Press coverage of the field has done little to resolve these problems. Consumer magazines and newspapers typically run somewhat breathless "gee whiz" articles about all the wonders AI will bring; computer trade publications, on the other hand, often provide little more than detailed new product specifications and uncritical reportage of the vendors' claims.

AI books, for their part, have mostly fallen into two categories: textbooks or technical investigations of AI, and philosophical treatises deliberating the nature of human intelligence and the feasibility of machine thought. Little, if anything, has been published to address the interests and concerns of the general business community, which stands to be the group most affected by the near-term commercialization of AI. Dwight Davis and I wrote this book in an attempt to fill this void. In the process, we believe we have produced an overview of AI that can serve as a general introduction to the technology and its implications.

Given that the bulk of our readers may have little direct experience with computers, we have tried to avoid the use of technical jargon or concepts that may be unfamiliar whenever possible. We do believe, however, that a basic understanding of how AI works will prove both interesting and important to the reader. If nothing else, such an understanding will help cut through the aura of mystique that often surrounds the field. Our examination of AI technology centers on two of its most promising areas: natural language processing and expert (or knowledge-based) systems. By gaining insight into how a computer can understand English questions or can help make a medical diagnosis, the reader will be better able to evaluate the limits and the potential of AI.

Grasping the commercial implications of artificial intelligence requires more than familiarity with its underlying technology. The rapidity with which AI-based products will emerge is intimately tied to such related issues as the quality of computer science education, the availability of skilled researchers, and the amount of money and talent devoted to basic research and product development. As such, our book goes beyond a mere recitation of the fundamentals of AI technology. It also examines the status of AI instruction within our institutes of higher education; it compares the respective approaches to this marketplace by the United States and its major competitor, Japan; and it projects what can be expected of the technology over the next several years. In short, the book attempts to look not just at the "how-to" of AI, but also at the environment in which it is nurtured and at the marketplace in which it must compete.

This book represents the opinion of both of the authors. Although I am president and CEO of Artificial Intelligence Corporation and author of the *Intellect* natural language system, I've made every attempt to avoid such a slanted approach, and have tried to present representative ideas and products that differ from my own. But removing all bias from the book is not my intent. It's because I have had the experience of developing and commercializing an AI product that I believe I can write on the subject with some authority. If I subjugated all my opinions in a quest for a perfectly balanced presentation, I think the reader would be shortchanged rather than rewarded.

I feel able to comment on the state of computer science education at the university level because of my own experience as a college professor. My perspectives on the pitfalls that often claim as victims those who try to commercialize AI research were formed during the years I spent making the transition from the academic community to the world of venture-funded entrepreneurs. And my comments about what types of products are likely to succeed or fail in the unforgiving marketplace are based on my experience in developing and selling an AI-based product.

In the book I occasionally refer to the *Intellect* product to illustrate technical points about natural language processing. My intent is to simply use the system I know best as an example of some of the concepts I would otherwise have to discuss in the abstract.

Finally, I have sidestepped the philosophical debate about whether machines can, or will ever, think. While a fascinating topic for speculation, the issue of machine intelligence can obscure the very real advances being achieved through the use of AI. Every person will have to come to their own conclusion as to whether or not these advances produce thinking computers. In the meantime, however, AI-based computers are already performing tasks far beyond the capabilities of any previous machines. Realizing the potential of these computers, and understanding their limits, will be one of the most critical requirements for individual computer users and for the business community at large. I hope this book can serve to make this task a manageable one.

LARRY R. HARRIS

1

AI Comes of Age

- The Meaning of Intelligence
- A Whirlwind Evolution
- The Roots of AI
- A Market Ripe for AI
- Computers as Tools

Many people approach computers with a mixture of distrust, skepticism, and even fear—and for good reason. The typical computer is idiosyncratic and hard to use, knowledge about one machine is often useless when applied to another, and what initially seemed to be a very smart contraption sometimes seems more like a very dumb annoyance. Still, most people who work with computers eventually overcome their initial misgivings and, after a fair amount of effort, come to appreciate electronic processors as powerful and useful tools.

Now, a fascinating computer science discipline called artificial intelligence promises to topple many of the barriers that exist between people and computers. Artificial intelligence (AI) is just beginning to appear in commercial products after almost 30 years of research and development in university and corporate labs. The discipline encompasses a broad spectrum of fields and little agreement exists as to what, exactly, "artificial intelligence" means. But one common thread unites the developers of this technology: They are attempting to imbue computers with traits long regarded as specific, and unique, to human beings. The targeted traits include understanding and speaking natural languages, such as English, the ability to give expert advice about fields as diverse as medicine and geology and, generally, to exhibit behavior that we normally associate with human thought and intelligence.

Intelligent computers? Is nothing sacrosanct? Aren't computer scientists aware of all the bleak scenarios that have been drawn by science fiction writers and film makers about future computers running amok?

Are some people so unable to separate fact from fancy that they actually believe that an electronic machine could ever match the intricate and mysterious workings of the human mind?

Such questions are common, but not everyone views artificial intelligence with trepidation or skepticism. As in the field of genetic engineering, potential for abuse exists in the pursuit of AI. But, just as genetic engineers believe the potential benefits of their research outweigh most of the risks, those developing artificial intelligence believe their work holds much promise. The public perception of this work, however, is often laden with misconceptions about the field and miscalculations about its likely role in our world.

No doubt the most common source of AI awareness is science fiction. For decades, writers have created future worlds populated by intelligent computers and robots; the resulting roles that humans play are usually less-than-happy ones. With assembly line robots already replacing people in some manufacturing plants, such fantasy worlds seem, at times, uncomfortably close to reality. Yet, deep down, people tend to draw a line between the proven ability of robots to perform rote, manual labor, and the potential for computers to one day handle tasks that require "true" intelligence. Yet, despite what most believe, that line is not inviolable.

The Meaning of Intelligence

Computers already routinely perform tasks that would have been labeled intelligent several years ago. However, "intelligence" is a poorly understood concept. Few contemplate what it means, and those who do rarely agree on a definition. Because so many definitions of intelligence exist, it's possible to keep demanding increasingly stringent requirements for the demonstration of machine thought, requirements that always stay one step ahead of what state-of-the-art computers can accomplish.

For example, creating a computer that could play world-class chess was once a Holy Grail for those seeking to develop intelligent machines. Today a number of chess-playing computer programs demonstrate a mastery of the game that falls just short of the Grand Master level, but this capability is somehow no longer a definitive demonstration of machine thought. Because chess-playing computers use well-understood, human-programmed techniques to achieve their success, and because these techniques differ from the methods human players employ, few believe that such computers really "think."

Ironically, the claim that machines can exhibit intelligence has precipitated an unprecedented effort to understand the workings of the human mind. The field of artificial intelligence is unique in this regard because it provides proofs as well as theories. AI is hardly the first or the foremost discipline to examine questions about human intelligence and behavior. Psychology, philosophy, and linguistics are among the long-standing players in this game. But by their nature, these fields consist almost solely of developing theories about the workings of the human mind. And, despite the fact that there has been no adequate way to test the accuracy of these theories, many have become accepted "facts" within their respective realms.

The early AI researchers, too, believed in the accuracy of many of these theories. These researchers were charged with implementing the theories on machines in order to imitate human behavior, but things didn't go as smoothly as expected. For example, when computer scientists first started to program machines to understand English, the scientists thought the task before them was relatively straightforward. After all, they had in hand theories of language and grammar that had been developed and refined over hundreds of years. All that needed to be done was to program these theories and rules into the computer and Voilá! A machine that understands English. But when the scientists programmed the accepted rules and theories they failed. Many theories simply didn't hold up when they were tested, a test that was never feasible prior to the availability of computers.

In fact, in almost every theoretical field involved with studying human thought and behavior, major holes were discovered as AI researchers attempted to use the theories to program machines. Many bedrock concepts were found to be devoid of the capability to fulfill their expected roles. As a result, AI has put a lot of pressure on the theoreticians in a number of fields. It's no longer enough to say

"Here's how I think people do this," or "Here's how I think it can be done." With the advent of AI, the theories can be embodied in electronic machines, and be shown to work or to fail. As such, the new methods employed by AI scientists as they push the frontiers of machine intelligence have also brought new vigor to the many associated disciplines relevant to their quest. Consequently, along with producing computers that contain the seeds of thought, AI is helping create a fascinating—and more accurate—window into our own minds.

Spurred on by AI, the scientific and philosophical debate about the nature of human and machine intelligence has become extremely vibrant. But the debate sometimes draws attention from the very real advances now occurring in AI. Regardless of whether these advances garner the "intelligence" label, they are certain to have a profound impact on our lives. And they will achieve this impact, often in surprisingly simple ways, by making computers exhibit skills long presumed to reside exclusively in the domain of human beings.

A Whirlwind Evolution

The theory of computing dates back more than a century, to when Charles Babbage postulated an "analytic" machine and Ada Lovelace performed what is commonly regarded as the first machine programming. But it was only four decades ago that the first modern computer was constructed. Developed in secrecy by J. Presper Eckert and John Mauchly at the University of Pennsylvania during World War II, the ENIAC computer was publicly unveiled in 1946. In the 40 years since, computer scientists have amazed the world with an astonishing succession of rapid advances.

Foremost among the computer milestones have been developments in the actual device machinery, or hardware. In fact, so-called "generations" of computers have been measured primarily by specific hardware advances. The 1960s creation of the transistor replaced the first-generation vacuum tubes. The development of integrated circuits on a semiconductor chip in the 1970s; and the continued shrinking of electronic components through large-scale integration (LSI), which became practical only several years ago, led to further generations. The last, LSI, has brought us to the current "fourth generation" of computers.

This generation is characterized by a diverse group of computing machines. Inexpensive microprocessor chips no bigger than a fingernail already squeeze the equivalent of hundreds of thousands of transistors onto their tiny surfaces. Supercomputers costing millions of dollars have attained processing speeds of half-a-billion operations per second, and can perform in minutes tasks that once took months, or were totally intractable. In what promises to be the first step in the long-predicted arrival of computing for the masses, personal computers have begun to proliferate throughout our businesses, homes, and schools.

While hardware advances will continue to play a crucial role in the evolution of computers, the relative importance of software, the programs that orchestrate the operation of the machine circuitry, has grown dramatically. Just as hardware has progressed through various evolutionary stages, so has software seen several distinct generations. Software languages have evolved independently of the computer hardware advances, but, coincidentally, these languages are also now at the fourth generation. As it happens, the emerging fifth generation of each is critical to the advancement of AI.

Computer hardware improvements promise to deliver incredibly powerful machines at a fraction of the cost of today's fastest supercomputers. As such, all fields of computer science stand to benefit, since more powerful machines mean faster processing, larger memories for storing information, and the ability to manipulate this information in ways not practical before. But of all the computer sciences, artificial intelligence stands to benefit the most from improved computers. Not only will the new machines permit the faster execution of complex AI programs, they will also serve as development aids that researchers can exploit as they delve further into the subtleties of machine thought. Despite the leverage next-generation hardware will provide, however, the immediate future of AI is primarily dependent upon the realm of software programming.

Software is crucial in the development of AI because it's the computer programs that direct the machines in their attempts to perform humanlike tasks. These tasks include inference and deduction and the use of rules-of-thumb, or "heuristics." In performing such operations, the software must also rely upon an extensive storehouse of information programmed into the computer's memory.

Combining the appropriate background information with various rules of reasoning permits computers to perform what is sometimes called "knowledge processing." Such processing represents a quantum leap beyond the "data processing" and "word processing" exhibited by most of today's computers. To a traditional computer, for example, the word "eagle" means nothing; its just a series of letters (which aren't even recognized as letters by the machine) entered by a human operator. Most people, on the other hand, have numerous associations for—or knowledge about—the word: it's the name of a large bird, it's the symbol of the United States, it's an endangered species, it's a skillful hunter of other animals, and on and on.

To move beyond traditional processing and achieve knowledge processing, the computer must also "understand" something of the relationships between different pieces of data. The knowledge important for a computer to understand is heavily dependent upon the tasks the computer must perform. The word "eagle" has no place in a system dedicated to accounting tasks; it may be sufficient for a natural language understanding computer to merely recognize the word as a noun with a specific definition; and a system designed to contain and manipulate ornithological information may store volumes of data associated with the word.

Of course, hundreds of books already contain such detailed information, and we never presume to label them intelligent. But when a computer uses its processing rules to discern relationships that aren't explicitly stated in its memory, or when it draws conclusions that are beyond the grasp of all but a few experts in the field—tasks within the reach of today's machines—the lines between human intelligence and computer knowledge processing begin to blur.

The Roots of AI

As a field, artificial intelligence got seriously underway in 1956 when a group of computer scientists convened the first AI conference at Dart-

mouth College. The organizers included John McCarthy (who is cred-
ited with coining the term "artificial intelligence"), Marvin Minsky of
MIT, Nathaniel Rochester of IBM, and Claude Shannon of Bell Laboratories. The youth of the overall computer field and the seemingly
boundless potential of AI combined to create an air of heady confidence in the early years of the new discipline.

Although the computers of the 1950s seem hopelessly inept when
compared to their modern counterparts, their capabilities seemed almost miraculous at the time. If these machines could perform numerical calculations at blinding speeds, why couldn't they perform a wide
variety of feats better and faster than human beings? Many of AI's
initial predictions for success were dashed, however, as the difficulties
of creating intelligent-acting computers gradually became apparent.

Although various researchers did achieve impressive results in narrow AI fields, some widely publicized experiments failed grandly. Most
notable of these was in the area of machine translation. It was thought
that properly programmed computers could become automatic translators of, say, Russian to English. Instead, the early machine translators
became subjects of ridicule, not respect, as their output often proved
more ludicrous than accurate. The machines simply made direct conver-
sions of words from one language to another without taking such
factors as the words' content and possible multiple meanings into
consideration.

Failures like those produced a general skepticism about all AI en-
deavors, a skepticism that seriously wounded the overall field. Virtually
overnight, AI researchers found their funding evaporating and their
professional support dwindling. Computer research continued full steam,
but only in such "practical" areas as semiconductors, computer languages, machine architectures, and peripheral devices. AI developers
had committed the cardinal sin of promising more than they could
deliver, at least given the available technology, and they paid for their
miscalculation. The research was abandoned by all but a few corporate
and university laboratories, and the remaining AI researchers often
labored under a reputation of being dreamers who simply couldn't
accept the limits of machines.

Now, after years of obscurity, AI is back in vogue. For the first time, products that employ artificial intelligence techniques are successfully entering the commercial market. In fact, the accepted benefits of AI are now so great that companies are falling over themselves to place the "artificial intelligence" label on their products, deserved or not. As recently as two or three years ago, such a label would have probably driven away more customers than it attracted. Today, the association with AI is perceived as being a potential gold mine. No doubt many AI scientists find it amusing that, after enduring their long-standing exile from computer science's limelight, they are suddenly much-sought-after gurus of computing's new wave.

A Market Ripe for AI

A number of factors combined in the late 1970s and early 1980s to prepare the way for AI's emergence from the labs. The proliferation of computers throughout businesses and homes placed the machines in the hands of people not skilled in their operation. The very increase in the numbers of installed computers helped create markets large enough to offset the substantial development costs usually associated with artificial intelligence products. Computers also entered factories where, in concert with programmable robots and other systems, they became responsible for conveying parts, assembling products, controlling inventories, and projecting demands. Meanwhile, noncomputerized fields grew in complexity, creating new types of opportunities for computers to exploit.

Artificial intelligence is not by any means a narrow field, and AI researchers work in a variety of specialized disciplines. Two main branches of AI have exerted the most impact on solving near-term problems. One, natural language processing, lets people use their own language—be it English, French, Japanese, or whatever—to communicate with computers. This capability eliminates the need to learn awkward computer languages, and gives a much broader range of people access to computers. So far, natural language understanding is essentially limited to words typed into a computer's keyboard, but it will eventually be extended to include spoken words.

The other AI branch, and the one that has received the most publicity, is that of expert systems. As the name implies, these systems contain the knowledge of experts in specific fields, along with the reasoning rules these people employ to manipulate their knowledge and arrive at conclusions. Given this capability, expert systems can serve as assistants to people, giving suggestions and opinions, and explaining the derivation of these if asked. The best-known expert systems include some in such fields as medical diagnosis, geological surveying, and, appropriately, computer system configuration. Natural language and expert systems are complementary, in that they can work in concert to produce a very-easy-to-use, very "smart" computer.

The power that AI techniques bring to computers is impressive, and the research that developed these techniques was, and is, long and arduous. But the actual functioning of AI-based computers is not difficult to understand. Since the machines use many of the methods employed in mathematics, the general concepts underlying their operation are surprisingly simple to grasp. It's just when the computer brings its great speed and memory into play that these relatively simple procedures produce hard-to-believe capabilities.

Still, the programming of computers with the rules and information needed to perform humanlike tasks at anywhere near the level of a person is a daunting job. As a result, many working in AI look askance at some of the products now claiming to incorporate artificial intelligence. The indignation felt by some researchers about the misuse of AI labels by less-than-deserving products goes beyond mere snobbishness about "true" AI. Rather, they fear that a surfeit of outlandish claims for AI may cause another backlash against the field if the claims fall flat. Many researchers believe artificial intelligence has almost boundless potential, but even its most ardent proponents admit that the realization of many AI capabilities will be a fairly slow process.

Market realities have added some speed to this process, however. Most notable in this regard is Japan's 10-year Fifth-Generation Project. Scheduled for completion in 1991, the project—which coordinates government, university and industrial research—has a goal of using AI and new hardware designs to take computers a quantum leap beyond anything existing today. If successful, the Japanese could become extremely strong competitors in the computer industry, although it's unlikely that success would bring them total market domination, as some fear.

As with any frontier research effort, it's difficult to assess the likely end results of the Japanese project. But one result has already become evident: The Fifth-Generation Project has stimulated the inception of hundreds of other AI projects around the world. Much of this activity, like that in Japan, is government supported. This is true in the United States, where the Defense Department's major research funding agency has plans to spend about $600 million over the first five years of a broad project intended, in part, to develop machine intelligence. Few expect or want the United States to totally mimic the Japanese strategy of coordinating a university, industry, and government triad to work on well-defined, mutual goals. Even with the massive growth of government-sponsored research in this area, start-up entrepreneurial firms and established computer companies will remain a crucial element in the furthering of artificial intelligence in this country.

Both the United States and Japan, not to mention the European countries active in AI, will likely realize a good measure of success in future years. The potential AI market is huge, and is certainly large enough to support numerous participants. If one company or country gets a jump in some areas, other competitors will lead in different AI fields. This is not to say that the research and development activity in Japan should be ignored. Far from it. But the doomsday alarms sounded by some about the United States' AI prospects often ignore this country's strong lead in artificial intelligence, and the amount and quality of ongoing U.S. research.

Nevertheless, problems do exist in the United States. Most notable is a shortage of AI talent and the resulting strain likely to be placed on universities. When any research field suddenly becomes a darling of the commercial world, universities suffer an exodus of talent. This exodus is especially severe in AI, where the existing pool of knowledgeable researchers is extremely small and the potential commercial gains very large. By its nature, artificial intelligence work takes two to three years for a single project. This means long-term commitments are required of researchers, be they in academia or industry, and people with the necessary combination of commitment and skill are very hard to find. If AI's success is not to be limited, we need to seriously consider the shortcomings of our educational system, which must produce large numbers of skilled graduates to meet the market's growing demands.

Computers as Tools

As grand, or as threatening, as AI's destiny may be, that destiny is still no more than a multihued vision. But AI won't wait for its ultimate incarnation before it begins affecting people's lives. Its ability to bridge the gap between people and computers is already becoming evident. In a world where more and more people have to deal with computers regularly, AI is playing the ironic role of removing the "artificialness" of these human–machine interactions.

Once all is said and done, after all, the result of AI programming is to make computers act more like people. Whether this phenomenon is viewed as magic, as sacrilege, or as good science, it makes our interaction with computers much easier and much more powerful. In fact, "artificial intelligence" is an unfortunate misnomer for a field that really makes computers seem much more *natural* to us than conventional machines.

In the near term, AI's main effect will be to make computers more "invisible." That is, AI will present the user with a familiar face that disguises the workings of the underlying technology. At the same time, AI programs and methods will allow computers to break free from their traditional roles as number crunchers and as repositories of data. AI computers will store knowledge—be it about birds, medicine, or grammar—and this capability will make them more powerful tools than any existing machines.

Of course, the very power that can make AI-based computers so useful can also give rise to suspicion and fear. Few people today feel threatened by machines that perform physical labor, but this was not always true. And computers that encroach more and more into the realm of our mental processes may create much more of a challenge to our sense of individual worth and uniqueness. Will AI engender the formation of present-day Luddites? And, if so, will they be working for a just cause?

Probably the answer to both questions is no. If anything, our world promises to grow more complex, and computers will constitute our primary weapon in coping with this complexity. The questions about AI are no longer "Can it work?" and "Will it have a role?," but "What of many possible roles will AI play?" and "How independent will we permit computers to become in fulfilling these chosen roles?" For instance, an expert system that assists a doctor in making a diagnosis is one thing, but a system that independently performs a diagnosis and prescribes a treatment is quite another.

Properly managed, artificial intelligence promises to enrich and broaden our lives, not to make them less meaningful or less secure. AI will become so pervasive, and its power to effect change so broad, that it behooves people to understand at least the fundamental tenets of the field. Given that understanding, AI no longer seems so mystical or so threatening. And, with such understanding, people play informed roles in helping direct the application of this amazing technology.

2

Foundations

- Computer Hierarchy
- Programming Languages
- Rule-Based Programming
- LISP and LISP Machines

A critical aspect of artificial intelligence involves the search to better understand how humans perform intelligent processes. Much like the sciences of psychology, philosophy, and sociology the study of artificial intelligence centers around the intelligent behavior of humans. As we've noted, AI differs from other sciences in that it simulates its theories on a computer. It is not enough to postulate the way in which it appears that people carry out intelligent tasks; in the field of AI, any such theory must be accompanied by a computer simulation of the theory.

The successful implementation of some ideas on machines should not, however, be regarded as a proof that humans carry out the tasks in a similar way. In some instances, the same performance goals can be achieved through the use of totally different methods, and it's often impossible to know which of the methods is the closest to that employed by people performing the same tasks. What AI accomplishes is to limit the set of acceptable theories to those that are computationally feasible.

This whole issue of simulating intelligent behavior on computers quite properly comes under some scrutiny in its own right. How can we simulate on a device built out of transistors an activity that we know takes place on neurons? These devices are so fundamentally different that many people feel that the results derived in one environment have no relationship to the other. But this argument misses the point that people carry out different levels of processing and that the higher levels of processing can be simulated independent of the lower levels.

Figure 2.1 illustrates the type of hierarchy involved. At the bottom level is the neuron structure that serves as the biological foundation for human intelligence. Based on this neural structure is some form of memory, both long and short term. Researchers are still groping for the exact mechanism by which neurons are able to store people's memories, but this doesn't mean that we can't study memory independent of the use of neurons as the storage media. In fact, it's easy to use electronic devices to simulate memory on the computer, thereby permitting the study of the higher level processing activities that are based on memory.

One way to categorize the different kinds of processing involved in intelligent behavior is shown in Figure 2.1. "Search" refers both to the activity of scanning memory for specific facts and to the trial-and-error process of evaluating several alternatives. "Planning" is the higher-level reasoning process involved in deciding what facts are relevant, or what alternatives should be evaluated. "Problem solving" refers to the

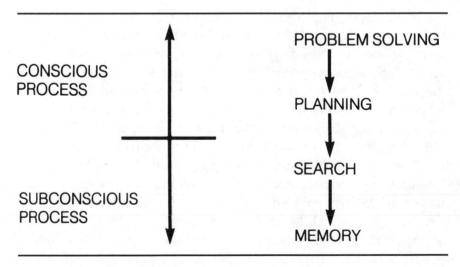

Figure 2.1   Levels of Processing

strategic analysis of how problems are broken into subproblems and how longer-term considerations are brought into play.

This hierarchy is not meant to be definitive, but to characterize the nature of the various processes involved and to show how one level can be isolated from the others. However, it does help to illustrate how little we really know about how humans perform any of these activities. What knowledge we do have is at the extremes of the diagram. From neurobiology we do know some of the basic facts about how neurons work. From conscious introspection we can determine how people plan and carry out simple examples of problem solving. Since human consciousness disappears somewhere between the search and planning levels, it is difficult to gain insights about how people actually perform search and memory functions.

Trying to understand human behavior from the bottom up, such as from the neurobiological level, can be dangerously misleading. Without having a reasonable understanding of the higher-level processes, it is very easy to incorrectly identify the functions of the lower-level components. Consider what might happen if a similar bottom-up approach was used to analyze the workings of a radio. After removing one of the resistors and hearing a howl, one might conclude that the function of the resistor was that of a "howl inhibitor." Similarly, if we view the radio as an unstructured combination of transistors, resistors, and capacitors we are unlikely to determine the high-level function of the total package. It is critical to recognize the functional role of the subassemblies of the amplifier, the tuner, and so on.

Computer Hierarchy

A hierarchy similar to the processing levels of people exists in computers that simulate intelligent behavior. As shown in Figure 2.2, the levels are the same except for the bottom level, which incorporates transistors or integrated circuits rather than neurons. The evolution of the computer has itself demonstrated the independence of the layers because the bottom-level devices upon which computers have been built have changed over the years. As illustrated in Figure 2.3, the underlying

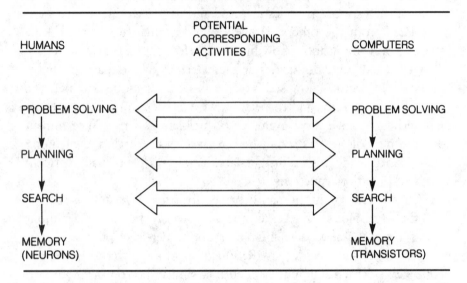

Figure 2.2   Levels of Processing

devices have undergone considerable change, from tubes to integrated circuits, without requiring a change in any of the higher-level processes.

As mentioned earlier, this hardware evolution has served as the primary basis for tracking the advancement of the computer. The first generation refers to the computers built from vacuum tubes. These machines were limited by slow switching speeds and by the rather high failure rate of the tubes. The use of the word "bug" to refer to a programming error actually began on first-generation computers when moths sometimes got trapped in the wiring and short circuited the devices. In those days, debugging was actually a physical activity!

The second-generation computers, based on transistors, were much faster and more dependable. The third generation (integrated circuits) was based on semiconductor chip technology that combined an entire circuit of transistors, resistors, and capacitors in a single device, rather than wiring separate devices together. Fourth-generation computers, the current state of the art, are based on a technology known as

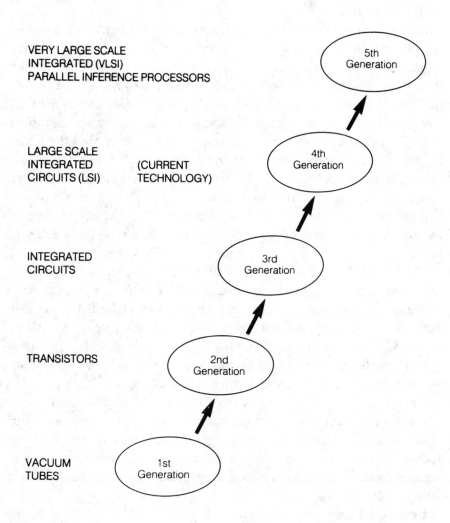

VERY LARGE SCALE
INTEGRATED (VLSI)
PARALLEL INFERENCE PROCESSORS

LARGE SCALE
INTEGRATED   (CURRENT
CIRCUITS (LSI)   TECHNOLOGY)

INTEGRATED
CIRCUITS

TRANSISTORS

VACUUM
TUBES

5th
Generation

4th
Generation

3rd
Generation

2nd
Generation

1st
Generation

Figure 2.3   Generations of Hardware

large-scale integration (LSI), which places larger, more-complex circuits on a single device. The fifth-generation computers, as defined by the Japanese, are based on very-large-scale integration (VLSI), but also encompass new computer architectures (parallel processing) and certain AI functions (inferencing).

Although much of the basis for human behavior remains a mystery, we can explain to any desired level of detail exactly how computers work. The basis of all computation is an electronic signal. Much like that controlling a household light, the electronic signal is either on or off. To represent even the smallest useful piece of information requires a sequence of electronic signals. This sequence is often represented by a string of 1s and 0s, which indicate the presence or absence of the signal in any given position. The computer's use of on/off signals permits computerized information to be represented by the binary number system, whose digits run 0 to 1 instead of 0 to 9 as they do in the decimal number system. Each binary digit, or "bit," carries one piece of information, indicated by the presence or absence of the electronic signal.

The binary, or base-two, number system uses a series of 1s and 0s to represent numbers equivalent to the more-familiar decimal system. Numbers in both systems can be written in an expanded form that takes into account their respective bases. For example, the decimal number 257 can be written as $(2 \times 10^2) + (5 \times 10^1) + (7 \times 10^0)$, with the powers of 10 derived from the decimal position of each digit. Likewise, the binary number 11011 can be written as $(1 \times 2^4) + (1 \times 2^3) + (0 \times 2^2) + (1 \times 2^1) + (1 \times 2^0)$. Thus, binary 11011 is equivalent to decimal 27. Because of the computer's on/off nature it can easily work with the binary strings and perform a full range of mathematical operations on them. The computer is also able to store alphabetic characters because various codes have been developed for representing each character as a string of 1s and 0s.

Because all computer information is stored and manipulated as sequences of 1s and 0s, it's relatively simple to create memory devices to accommodate this information. Such devices need only be able to exist in two states, on or off. By wiring two transistors together in such a way as to create a *bistable* device we can "remember" what the last electronic signal was. With a few of these *flip-flop* devices the computer can store a short sequence of electronic signals that represents a number or a letter; by combining hundreds of thousands of such devices—which may occupy no more than a single semiconductor chip thanks to VLSI technology—the machine's memory can hold volumes of information. Memory, at this level at least, is easy to understand. Even complex information and detailed machine instructions are, in the end, stored at this bit-by-bit level.

The mystique of the computer comes in as we move up the hierarchy toward more complex computational processes. Even a relatively simple process such as adding two numbers together can seem magical when performed at electronic processing speeds. Every computer has an "add" circuit whose function is to add binary numbers bit by bit. The rate at which this addition occurs is based on the computer's clock speed, which is often measured in thousandths of a second. But if the clock's pulse signal is slowed to one signal per second, it's possible to actually watch on a display the digits of each binary number come into position for adding. But when the clock pulse rate is increased to 1000 times a second, what was an obvious operation suddenly develops a mystique. The entire process seems completely understandable. The speed of the process by itself is enough to make a totally intelligible operation seem mysterious. In a similar way, the astonishing capabilities that AI brings to computers can, upon slowing them down and dissecting them, be perfectly understandable.

Programming Languages

Like the evolution of computer hardware, the languages with which the computers are given their instructions have also changed. In many respects the improvements in these programming languages have been even more radical than the admittedly astonishing hardware advances. It's important to appreciate the nature of the changes that occurred between each generation of programming language to understand how artificial intelligence fits into the picture at the just-emerging fifth-

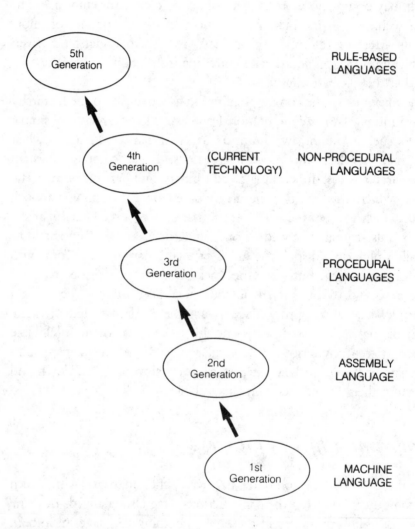

Figure 2.4   Generations of Software

generation level. A definition of some of the relevant terminology will help in this process.

"Programming" is simply the act of giving instructions to the computer. A "programming language" defines the set of rules that dictate the manner in which the instructions are given. In many cases the differences in programming languages are merely syntactic variations; if so, the choice between two such languages is largely a matter of taste. However, the differences between each generation of programming languages (Figure 2.4) are more profound. Essentially, each generation's languages allow communication with the machine at a different level of detail or "level of abstraction." That is, one instruction of a higher-level language may be equivalent to several hundred instructions of one of the lower-level languages.

"Machine language" is the language of 0s and 1s that is actually used by the machine directly. In truth, there is even a lower-level language called "microcode" that is used to construct the machine language. But even machine language is too detailed to be of much use to most people. It is simply too difficult to make much sense out of a stream of 0s and 1s printed across a page (Figure 2.5).

```
1001 0000 0010 0100    1101 0000 0000 1100    0000 0000 0000 0000 1100
0101 1000 0100 0001    0000 0000 0000 1000    0000 0000 0000 0000 1000
0101 1000 0100 0100    0000 0000 0000 0000    0000 0000 0000 0000 0000
0101 1000 0011 0001    0000 0000 0000 0000    0000 0000 0000 0000 0000
0101 1000 0011 0011    0000 0000 0000 0000    0000 0000 0000 0000 0000
0101 1000 0010 0001    0000 0000 0000 1100    0000 0000 0000 0000 1100
0101 1000 0010 0010    0000 0000 0000 0000    0000 0000 0000 0000 0000
0100 0001 0010 0010    0000 0000 0000 0111    0000 0000 0000 0000 0111
1000 1000 0010 0000    0000 0000 0000 0011    0000 0000 0000 0000 0011
0100 0100 0010 0000    1111 0000 0011 1010    0000 0000 0000 0011 1010
0101 1000 0011 0001    0000 0000 0000 0100    0000 0000 0000 0000 0100
0101 1000 0011 0011    0000 0000 0000 0000    0000 0000 0000 0000 0000
0100 0100 0010 0000    1111 0000 0100 0000    0000 0000 0000 0100 0000
1001 1000 0010 0100    1101 0000 0000 1100    0000 0000 0000 0000 1100
0000 0111 1111 1110
```

Figure 2.5 Machine Language

This difficulty in working with machine language prompted the creation of the second-generation "assembly language," which essentially established English mnemonics for each of the machine language instructions. That is, for each assembly language instruction there is a corresponding machine language instruction (Figure 2.6). This introduced some level of clarity to what had been incomprehensible sequences of machine language 1s and 0s. The "assembler," which converts assembly language to machine language, carries out that substitution as well as handling hundreds of other little details that make programming in assembly language tolerable.

```
*         NAME-BITOR
BITOR1    CSECT
          ENTRY  BITOR              COMMENTS
          USING  *,R15
BITOR     STM    R2,R4,12(R13)
          L      R4,8(R1)           GET PTR TO 3RD ARG
          L      R4,0(R4)           POINT TO 3RD ARG
          L      R3,0(R1)           GET PTR TO 1ST ARG
          L      R3,0(R3)           POINT TO 1ST ARG
          L      R2,12(R1)          POINT TO LENGTH
          L      R2,0(R2)           GET LENGTH
          LA     R2,7(R2)           ADD 7 FOR ROUNDING
          SRL    R2,3               DIVIDE BY 8 (LENGTH IN BYTES)
          EX     R2,MVCINST         MOVE 1ST ARG INTO 3RD
          L      R3,4(R1)           GET PTR TO 2ND ARG
          L      R3,0(R3)           POINT TO 2ND ARG
          EX     R2,OCINST          AND 2ND ARG WITH 3RD
          LM     R2,R4,12(R13)
          BR     R14
          DS     0H
MVCINST   MVC    0(0,R4),0(R3)
OCINST    NC     0(0,R4),0(R3)
          REGEQU
          END
```

Figure 2.6   Assembly Language Equivalent to Machine Language in Figure 2.5

A major advance took place in progressing from assembly language to the third-generation "procedural" languages. The first such language was FORTRAN. Each statement in FORTRAN could easily generate several hundred machine-language instructions. The third-generation languages provided a far more productive means of instructing the computer. A number of improved programming languages appeared within this generation. Among them are COBOL, BASIC, PL/1 (Figure 2.7), Pascal, and C. The vast majority of programs in use today are written in one of these languages. As always, though, everything written in a higher-level language must be translated to the 1s and 0s understood by the machine. The programs that convert the third-generation languages into machine language are called "compilers" if the program is completely translated before being run and "interpreters" if the translation is done on-the-fly while the program is being executed.

```
ON ENDFILE(EMPLOYEE_FILE) GOTO WRAP_UP;
PUT SKIP LIST ('1986 MAY ACT SALES',
               '1986 MAY EST SALES',
               'DIFFERENCE', '% CHANGE');
DO WHILE ('1'B);
  READ FILE(EMPLOYEE_FILE)
    INTO(EMPLOYEE_ RECORD)'
  IF EMPLOYEE_RECORD.DEPT='MEN'
  / EMPLOYEE_RECORD.DEPT='WOMEN'
  THEN DO;
    DIFFERENCE = Y1986_MAY_ACT_SALES -
      Y1986_ MAY_EST_SALES;
    CHANGE = 100 * DIFFERENCE
      Y1986_MAY_
      EST_SALES;
    PUT SKIP LIST (Y1986_MAY_ACT_SALES,
      Y1986_ MAY_EST_SALES, DIFFERENCE, CHANGE);
    END;
  END;
WRAP_UP: ;
```

Figure 2.7   Third-Generation Programming Language PL/1

All of the languages up through the third generation require that the programmer define a precise sequence of the steps or "algorithm" that the computer must follow. Each step is precisely described, leaving no room for judgment on the computer's part. The programs are complete descriptions not only of what the programmer wants done, but also exactly how to do it. This concept changed with the introduction of "non-procedural" or fourth-generation languages.

The fourth-generation languages take the approach of letting the programmers specify what they want accomplished and leaving it to the computer to figure out how to do it. This radical departure from the previous three generations has increased the productivity of programmers by a factor of 10 or more. Figure 2.8 shows a fourth generation language program for the same problem illustrated in Figure 2.7, which required nearly a page of PL/1, not to mention the corresponding amount of machine language. The most popular fourth-generation languages are FOCUS, RAMIS, and NOMAD. The key to their success is that they allow programmers to work at a much higher level of abstraction, much closer to the actual problem being solved, without having to constantly worry about the low-level details of how to express the problem to the computer.

```
PRINT 1986_MAY_ACT_SALES, 1986_MAY_EST_SALES,
      (1986_MAY_ACT_SALES _ 1986_MAY_EST_SALES),
      (100 * (1986_MAY_ACT_SALES _
      1986_MAY_EST_SALES) / 1986_MAY_ACT_SALES)
WHERE (DEPT = 'MEN' OR DEPT = 'WOMEN');
```

Figure 2.8   Fourth Generation Language Equivalent to Figure 2.7

The fifth-generation programming languages are just coming into being. As such, the exact nature of these languages is yet to be defined, but the basis of the fifth-generation languages is something referred to as "rule-based programming." The best examples of these languages are so-called "toolkit" products that some vendors are now selling to customers so that they can attempt to write their own AI programs. This new approach to programming does not specify a sequence of steps to the computer, but rather a set of rules. The computer determines the appropriate time to make use of one of the rules. The improvement in programmer productivity effected by the fifth-generation languages has not been determined. However, it appears that certain types of problems, particularly artificial intelligence problems, that were largely intractable for the earlier generations are possible with the rule-based approach. For example, natural language systems (Figure 2.9) can be implemented using the rule-based approach.

FOR THE MEN'S AND WOMEN'S
DEPARTMENTS, COMPARE THE ACTUAL AND
FORECASTED SALES FOR LAST MONTH.

Figure 2.9   Natural Language Request Equivalent to Figure 2.8

As programming languages have evolved, the improvements realized have gradually changed from a quantitative increase in productivity to a qualitative change in the nature of the types of problems that could be effectively solved. At some level, of course, all the languages eventually produce a sequence of machine-language instructions. However, much like the firing of neurons, this is too low a level of detail. The important issue is the effectiveness of the process by which programmers can express problems to the computer. The higher-level languages allow this process to take place in a far more effective fashion. In a sense, the goal of the fifth generation is to make this process so straightforward that even users not technically trained in the art of programming will be able to easily give instructions to the machines.

One final point is worth noting in our examination of programming languages: There is tremendous variation in the use of the languages within the third generation. Some, such as COBOL, are appropriate for business data processing; others, such as FORTRAN, for numerical analysis; and others are best suited for similarly restricted tasks. For example, all of the fourth- and fifth-generation language processors (the programs that translate the languages into machine language) are written in third-generation languages, much like the first FORTRAN compiler had to be written in assembly language.

This seems like a contradiction. If the higher-level programming languages are so great, why don't we use them for everything? The answer is that the increased leverage of the higher-level languages comes at the price of a narrower range of application. Assembly language remains the most general-purpose language. For each level that you move up, some areas of application are sacrificed. The fourth-generation languages are targeted at business data processing and decision support applications; it would not be appropriate to implement a telecommunications system in such a language. Therefore, it is necessary to take into account the nature of the program being written before choosing the best language to use. In general, it is best to use the highest-level language appropriate to the problem at hand.

Rule-Based Programming

Rule-based programming—the new programming metaphor of the fifth-generation languages—happens to be well-suited for use in attacking the high-level problems addressed by artificial intelligence. Rather than providing a precise step-by-step set of instructions to the computer, the rule-based approach specifies a set of rules to be applied. The execution process then becomes one of searching for a sequence of rules that will solve the given problem. The main characteristic of this generation is thus the change from a temporal connection of instructions to a logical connection among rules. The computer will deal with applying the rules in the correct order. The programmer can enter the rules in any order, unlike ordinary instructions, which must be specified in the particular sequence that they are to be executed.

The most successful, commercial rule-based languages are KEE, ART, and S.1. These products provide editing capabilities for entering, altering, and deleting rules; the inference engine for applying the rules; debugging aids to facilitate programming; and a host of graphic output facilities. It should be emphasized that the rule-based approach to solving AI problems is only one of those developed in AI research over the past 30 years. These include object-oriented programming, generate and test, and constraint propagation, among others. Rule-based

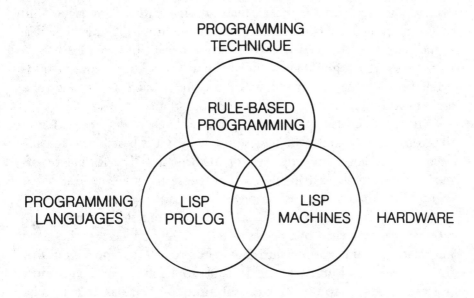

Figure 2.10   Overlap of Rule-Based Programming of Natural Language and
                    Expert Systems

programming is given special treatment here because it is the technological foundation of the two AI applications that have entered the
marketplace: natural language processing and expert systems. A rough
estimation of the relative degree of importance of this programming
technique for these two applications is depicted in Figure 2.10.

   The intended value of this approach is twofold. First, it is believed
that this new programming methodology will allow us to solve a
variety of problems that have been too difficult to solve with third- or
fourth-generation approaches. Second, the hope is that nonprogrammers
who are experts in their own specialties could enter the rules relevant to
these specialties and, in effect, become the programmers. One could
imagine the ideal application of this technology being doctors building
a medical diagnosis application on their own. This would represent
successful attainment of both goals, with nonprogrammers creating a
system that was previously beyond the talents of even skilled program-

mers working with earlier generation languages. While there is some evidence to support the belief that fifth-generation languages will, indeed, permit the solving of once intractable problems, this benefit is by no means an accepted fact. The second benefit of turning nonprogrammers into programmers is not yet practical with the current fifth-generation languages. Whether it will become possible as the languages are refined is still very much of an open question.

Although rule-based programming is a relatively recent innovation in the world of computers, the tenets upon which it is based have actually been around since the early days of mathematics. The formal proofs most of us experienced in high school geometry involved rule-based logic. Mathematics itself is simply an association of formal rules to some notion of truth in nature. A proof that something is true is no more than a sequence of rules (theorems) being applied to the given information to transform it into the desired result. It is interesting that this one activity of humans that demands so much insight and instinct is actually reduced to the mindless substitution of characters according to some very simple rules.

In essence, rule-based programming is the establishment of a theorem-proving application, but without the rigor necessary in mathematics. That is, the program attempts to find a sequence of rules that will "prove" the target problem, but the rules don't have to exhibit the logical consistency required in mathematics. The rules need not always be true. The rules may not always apply. The problem we are trying to solve may not be, strictly speaking, true in all circumstances. To solve real-world problems, rule-based programming uses the basic concepts of mathematical theorem proving, without the rigor of pure mathematics.

This definition may at first seem to paint the rule-based approach in a harsh light. But an unfortunate fact of life is that the solutions to most real-world problems are not provable in any formal system. Therefore, if we want to solve practical problems, we must loosen up the constraints somewhat, while still using the basic mechanism developed for mathematical logic. The net effect is that the results we obtain will be no better than the accuracy of the rules we put in, but at least we stand a chance of solving some important problems that have so far been beyond the reach of computers.

Essentially rule-based programming consists of three components: facts, rules, and an "inference engine." The rules are used to transform the facts relevant to a particular problem into the desired conclusion. The inference engine is responsible for determining which rules to apply and in what order.

The practical experience gained to date in using the rule-based approach is limited. Contrary to some of the write-ups in the popular press, the successful commercial application of this technology is still very small. While some impressive AI prototype products have been built, only a precious few are "in production" and in daily use within companies. However, given the current development activity, we can expect to see the number of applications in production to grow rapidly.

In general, it appears that the rule-based technology is appropriate, and perhaps even necessary, to solve certain types of problems, such as natural language analysis. More experience is needed prior to evaluating the rule-based paradigm as a general-purpose approach to programming. It's true that the classic bugs that occur in traditional programs when instructions are placed out of sequence do not occur in free-form, rule-based programs. Instead, bugs occur due to the logical connectivity of the rules not being correct. Neither kind of bug is necessarily "better" than the other, and both require rather extensive diagnostic skills on the part of the programmer to track down and eventually fix. There is the possibility that within the rule-based approach the debugging activity itself could be automated by a supervisory-level computer system.

Debugging aids already exist that try to identify logical inconsistencies introduced as new rules are added. If these debugging aids improve beyond their current capabilities of catching only simple inconsistencies, it would provide a major boost to the goal of having nontechnically trained users actually write their own rule-based programs.

The subtle interactions that can take place among the rules constitute the biggest drawback to the rule-based approach, and make it clear why the fifth-generation shouldn't be viewed as a panacea to the problems of programming. In all fairness it must be said that a very similar problem exists with third- and fourth-generation programs. For instance, studies done on large programs written in third-generation languages indicated that it took an average of ten attempts for trained programmers to fix one bug without introducing another. Programming is simply not an easy task, with any generation language. But as we will now see, the rule-based approach is making impressive strides in tackling difficult AI problems. The requirements raised in bringing human traits to computers fit naturally into the logical format of the fifth-generation languages.

LISP and LISP Machines

At this point it is useful to position the AI rule-based programming metaphor relative to two other important AI concepts: AI programming languages such as LISP and PROLOG, and specialized AI computers such as LISP machines.

LISP is a high-level programming language developed in the 1950s that serves as an excellent basis for implementing rule-based programs. PROLOG, a more recent language that allows "PROgramming with LOGic," is even more closely associated with the rule-based approach. Virtually all development of AI programs has taken place in one of these two languages. The reasons most often cited for this fact are the ease with which prototypes can be built with these languages and their built-in features like flexible data structures and storage management, which free programmers from a host of otherwise tedious tasks.

In the case of LISP, the excellent development environment that has been built up around the language over the years may be as useful as the language itself. This development environment provides extremely powerful editing facilities and debugging aids that help to make up for some weaknesses in the language itself. In fact, the rapid prototyping capability common with LISP projects is probably due more to its development tools than to the language itself. Because these tools are not part of the LISP language, they could theoretically be applied to PROLOG or even to more-conventional programming languages such as C or PL/1.

LISP machines are specialized computers that implement the LISP

programming language in hardware and provide an exceptionally powerful implementation of the LISP development environment. The large
address space of the machines, their built-in storage management capabilities, and their rich use of graphics combine to make them an almost
ideal facility with which to develop AI programs. Some PROLOG
proponents, particularly those in Japan, are following the LISP machine lead and are building PROLOG machines to better exploit that
language.

It's important to understand, however, that rule-based programming,
AI languages such as LISP and PROLOG, and LISP (or PROLOG)
machines are all independent concepts, as illustrated in Figure 2.11.
For example, it is certainly possible to implement rule-based programs
in the C programming language on an IBM computer. The use of a
LISP machine or even of the LISP language is not required.

The middle section of Figure 2.11 shows the intersection of all three
concepts, namely performing rule-based programming in LISP on a

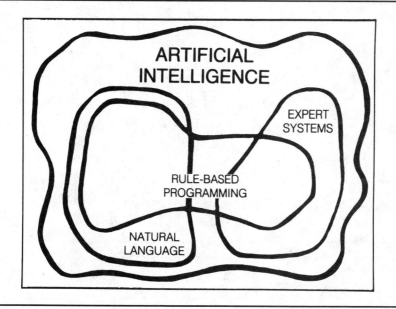

Figure 2.11 "Rule-Based" Programming Can Be Done Independently of
Programming Language and Hardware

LISP machine. This is an extremely effective approach, but by no means a requirement. In fact, real-world constraints such as equipment cost or the presence of needed data on an IBM mainframe may rule out the use of a LISP machine. Furthermore, the use of high-level system languages, such as S.1, ART, or KEE, establish a level of rule-based programming that is independent of LISP and can therefore run outside the LISP environment as well as on non-LISP hardware.

For these reasons, we can expect to see more and more AI systems being developed independent of LISP and delivered on conventional computers. The LISP machines will be used for developing some new systems and for delivering certain standalone applications, but over time the bulk of AI programs will run on general-purpose hardware.

3
Natural Language Processing

- Natural Language History
- Syntax—Rules of Grammar
- Semantics—Shades of Meaning
- Pragmatics—Determining Intent
- Level of Semantic Primitives
- Solving the Entire Problem
- Conceptual View
- Ambiguity
- Aggregates
- Summarization
- Data-Analysis Capability
- Speech

Teaching computers to understand English has been a goal and dream of computer researchers since the 1950s. It was one of the earliest problems addressed by the field of artificial intelligence because natural language capability is perhaps the most fundamental talent that separates human intelligence from that of other animals. "Natural language" is a technical term for the languages used by people to communicate with one another. English, French, German, and Japanese are examples of natural languages. Before the creation of the formal computer languages there was no need to distinguish natural languages from any other, because natural languages were the only ones we had. (An exception to this rule is the "language" of mathematics, which, as were formal computer languages, developed to address certain detailed requirements not handled well by the natural languages.)

The advent of computers and the need to instruct them prompted the creation of the formal computer languages for two reasons. First, the computers simply were not capable of understanding natural languages; second, the precise nature of the instructions being given did not lend itself to natural language. Therefore, a number of formal computer languages were created to allow the precise specification of a sequence of machine instructions. These languages have served us well for the relatively low-level tasks that computers have been performing over the past 30 years.

More recently, as computers have been applied to higher-level tasks such as business problem solving, the nature of the communication has changed from a precise procedural orientation to a nonprocedural orientation. This evolution in our use of computers has affected the design of formal computer languages. The fourth-generation computer languages are a reflection of the higher-level interaction that is now taking place.

But this change in the level of use has eliminated one of the reasons why formal computer languages were created in the first place: the precise specification of low-level tasks. This doesn't present any problems, however, since the tasks encompassed by AI are high-level functions that don't require the specification of the nitty-gritty details. Therefore, the use of natural language for higher-level tasks is not only appropriate, but is also desirable for making computers more accessible to nontechnical users. Given all this, the only remaining difficulty is that computers, unlike people, don't magically learn natural language as they grow older.

The phenomenon of natural language is particularly interesting because virtually all people, across an enormous range of IQs, learn at least one such language. It is a process that we know very little about, yet everyone is an expert. For some reason, the ability of humans to learn natural languages diminishes after age 5 or 6. Learning a new natural language after that age typically becomes a much more difficult, conscious activity. We have yet to master the teaching of natural languages to adults. The structure and rules for natural languages are only partially understood. Books containing the rules on English grammar have far more exceptions than rules.

Given that it is difficult to teach adults new natural languages, with the specialized biological hardware that we all have for language processing, it is no surprise that teaching computers to understand English is an extremely difficult task. It is also a problem of enormous scientific interest because of its relationship to human language processing. Finally, it is a problem of great commercial value, because of the large numbers of people who wish to access the information in computers, but know only their natural language and not any of the formal computer dialects.

Natural Language History

The field of linguistics is the study of natural languages as used by people. The field of "computational linguistics" studies the use of natural language on computers. Not surprisingly, the two fields have a lot in common. Both are concerned with the underlying structure of natural languages and the rules governing their use. The early computer implementations of natural language systems relied almost entirely on standard linguistic theories. Even though today's natural language systems are still largely based on rather classical linguistic theory, we have learned a good deal more.

The early attempts to build natural language systems that could perform automatic translation from one natural language to another were straightforward implementations of the grammar books that had been used by people so successfully for many years. Unfortunately, these rules were not subject to the same precise interpretation by people as they were by computers. The results were so disastrous that government funding of this research area—substantial at one time— came to a virtual standstill. One of the classic examples often cited of the work of that era is the attempt of one system to translate "The spirit is willing but the flesh is weak" into Russian. The result came out as "The vodka is good, but the meat is rotten." The brute force implementation of classical linguistic theory is simply insufficient to understand and properly translate this type of sentence.

After a number of failed attempts to solve natural language problems through the application of classical theories, it was recognized that the level of specification that is useful for human understanding of a problem is rarely sufficient for a computer solution of the problem. People are simply not very demanding in their use of linguistic tools. Facilities written for human consumption are often incomplete and even internally inconsistent! Apparently this does not diminish their utility to people, but it does cause major problems in computer implementations.

The best example of the distinction between a person's linguistic requirements and a computer's is illustrated by the use of a common dictionary. The dictionary is filled with circular definitions because all the words that are used in the definitions are themselves defined in the same dictionary. There are no "primitive" words upon which all the other definitions are based. This circularity causes no problems for people because they simply stop the chain when they know all the words that have been used in one of the definitions. The computer, on the other hand, cycles endlessly, following the chain of definitions around and around. The computer requires a dictionary in which all definitions make use of simpler, more basic words than the word being defined. With such a dictionary, eventually the computer will derive a definition consisting only of the basic "primitive" words that it has been programmed to understand. Whether or not people rely on such primitive definitions is not clear. All we know is that, for computers, a basic foundation of primitive words is necessary for language understanding.

All of this notwithstanding, the tools developed in linguistics have had tremendous impact on the field of computational linguistics. In fact, the formalization of the rule-based paradigm comes from the linguistic work of Noam Chomsky. His landmark theoretical work has had impact far beyond computational linguistics, from compiler implementation to expert systems. In his attempt to capture the rules of English grammar in a mechanical process, Chomsky created the basis upon which nearly all formal computer languages have been defined. Even though his original attempt was insufficient to capture all the idiosyncrasies of English, it has been an enormously useful tool for a variety of applications in computer science.

In the early 1970s, research in computational linguistics was revitalized because of the realization that semantics, or dealing with meaning, is required in addition to syntactic analysis. The predominant view of classical linguistics has been that syntax alone is sufficient to analyze English sentences. But to be useful, computer implementations must do more than analyze the structure of sentences. They must understand and process them as well. This need eventually resulted in the introduction of semantics into the process, and has led to a much more satisfactory level of English understanding by machines. The big distinctions between the failures of the 1950s and the successes of the 1970s was the inclusion of semantics into the language analysis process.

For database inquiry systems, the inclusion of semantics is quite feasible, because of the limited context in which the questions are posed. The subject matter is very constrained. An accounting system, for example, has no need to understand the semantics of medical terminology. The inclusion of semantics is prohibitive for translation systems in which the subject matter is unconstrained. It's for this reason that certain uses of natural language are now commercially feasible, while other uses are still being researched.

The process of instructing a computer to understand a natural language such as English is difficult because of the inherent imprecision and ambiguity in the language. The programmer must address language's three basic components: syntax, semantics, and pragmatics. Syntactic analysis separates the English sentence into its constituent parts. This process helps the semantic analysis phase construct an internal representation for the meaning of the sentence. Pragmatic analysis goes one step beyond this by considering the intent of the speaker, not just considering a literal interpretation of the words that were used.

Syntax—Rules of Grammar

The first step in programming a computer to understand an English sentence is to determine the syntactic role played by each word in the sentence. The different meanings of "The boy hit the ball" and "The ball hit the boy" are due to the different roles played by the words in each sentence, since both sentences contain the same words. The syntactic analysis determines which word is the subject and which word is the direct object. The process of syntactic analysis is the same as "diagramming" sentences, as taught in grade school. Those readers who didn't enjoy the subject matter there may find the following discussion too detailed, and may want to skip to the next section.

In order to automate the diagramming process, it was necessary to formalize the representation of the rules of grammar and the diagramming structure to be more amenable to computerization. There are two very common ways of representing English grammar on a computer. These are a "context-free" grammar and an "augmented transition network" (ATN). The context-free grammar is the historic basis of the rule-based paradigm. It consists literally of replacement rules such as:

<sentence>	→	<verb phrase> <noun phrase>
<verb phrase>	→	[<adverb>] <verb> [<noun phrase>]
<noun phrase>	→	<adjective>* <noun> [<prep phrase>]
<prep phrase>	→	<prep> <noun phrase>
<noun><noun>	→	boy
<noun>	→	ball
<adjective><verb>	→	hit
<adjective>	→	the

where → indicates "replaced by"; < > indicates the syntactic categories (parts of speech); * means a sequence of 0 or more is allowed; and [ ] means the term is optional.

These rules, or "productions" as they are sometimes called, specify the legal constituents of each syntactic component. They are literally the "rules of grammar." The grammar consists of two parts: the structural rules and the dictionary definitions that show the roles that specific words can play.

If you start with <sentence> and continue replacing symbols bracketed by < >, according to the replacement rules, you will eventually generate a syntactically correct sentence. The sequence of rules used to derive a sentence is called its "derivation sequence." The purpose of a "parser" is to find the derivation sequence of the sentence being analyzed. This is the reverse of the derivation process.

Natural language analysis fits the rule-based paradigm of facts, rules, and inference engine as follows: The facts are the dictionary definition rules such as <noun> → boy. These simply tell the part of speech of each word. The rules are the rules of grammar. The inference engine is the parser that determines which rules to employ to construct the derivation sequence.

An ATN representing these same rules appears in Figure 3.1. Essentially, the ATN is just a visual representation of the context-free rules. The circles represent "states" of a simple machine, and the arcs represent the allowable "transitions" that the machine makes as it moves from one state to another. Each transition is labeled with the part of

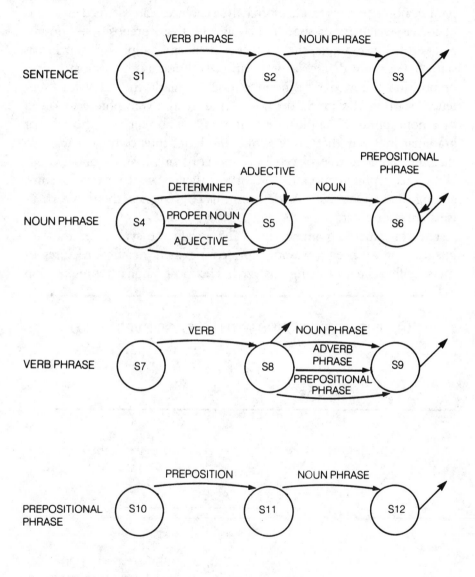

Figure 3.1   Augmented Transition Network Grammar

speech that is allowed to trigger the corresponding transition. In this way, the higher-level parts of speech (i.e., prepositional phrase, verb phrase, noun phrases, and, ultimately, sentences) are defined in terms of lower-level parts of speech such as adjectives, prepositions, nouns, and verbs. For example, the ATN for "prepositional phrase" starting at state S10 simply defines a prepositional phrase as the sequence of a preposition followed by a noun phrase. Similarly the ATN for "sentence" starting at state S1 defines a sentence as a verb phrase followed by a noun phrase. The purpose of the ATN is to represent the rules of grammar in a way that easily allows an input sentence to be parsed so that the syntactic role played by each word or phrase is understood. With this representation it is a little easier to see the relationships among the various rules. Aside from this convenience, the two formalisms are equivalent.

The context-free grammar or ATN specify the syntax for the languages, but we need a way of representing the syntactic structures of the specific sentences being analyzed. The most-familiar representation

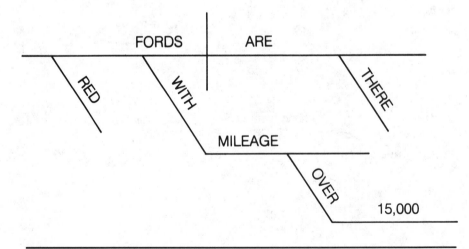

Figure 3.2   Sentence Diagram

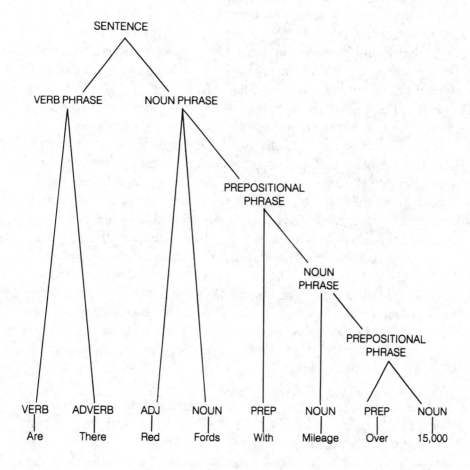

Figure 3.3   Parse Tree

is the diagramming structure taught in grade school (Figure 3.2). However, this structure is difficult to mimic on computers because of the myriad lines representing different relationships. A more appropriate formalism for computers is the "parse tree" shown in Figure 3.3. The parse tree shows the hierarchical relationship among the words by embedding them in a tree structure that indicates which words or phrases modify other words or phrases, as in the grammar school diagram.

To understand how the computer would use an ATN to syntactically parse a sentence, consider the example shown in Figure 3.3. First, each word in the sentence, "ARE THERE RED FORDS WITH MILEAGE OVER 15,000" is mapped to its part of speech, which corresponds to the bottom row of the parse tree. Now the ATN (Figure 3.1) is started at its initial state, S1, where it begins looking for a verb phrase. Processing at the sentence level pauses while processing at the verb phrase level proceeds from state S7. At this point, the verb "ARE" is parsed and the link from verb phrase to verb is created in the parse tree. Next the adverb "THERE" is parsed and the link from verb phrase to adverb is created in the parse tree. The upward arrow from state S9 then indicates that the system has successfully recognized a verb phrase and can now continue processing at the sentence level, now at state S2. This would cause the link from the sentence to verb phrase to be created in the parse tree. The processing would now continue with the word "RED" beginning a noun phrase. The remainder of the parse tree would be created in a similar fashion. A parse terminates successfully whenever the upward arc from state S3 is traversed, indicating that an entire sentence has been recognized.

The completed parse tree stores the syntactic relationship between each of the words in the sentence and acts as a road map for building the appropriate semantic structure for the sentence. It is important to recognize that the parse tree does not represent the meaning of the sentence. But without understanding a sentence's structure it is impossible to understand its meaning. For example, whether it is the boy or the ball that was hit in the earlier example.

Parse trees can be built in one of two ways, either top-down or bottom-up. The top-down parsers begin with the <sentence> symbol and apply the production rules in a forward order by replacing the category on the lefthand side of the rule by the contents of the right-hand side of the rule. The ATN is an example of a top-down parser. A bottom-up parser starts with the sentence and applies the production rules backwards. That is, it looks for the righthand of a rule and tries to replace it with the lefthand side. Eventually, the sentence will be reduced to the <sentence> symbol, if it was syntactically correct.

Syntactic analysis is the best understood aspect of computational linguistics. It is, in fact, the oldest and most studied example of rule-based programming. Over the years literally hundreds of "new" parsing techniques have been introduced in the AI literature. Some are more convenient than context-free and others are more efficient. Still, the most surprising fact is how little the basic concepts have changed in syntactic analyzers over the years. Most of the approaches are simply variations on Chomsky's original theme.

Because syntactic analysis is relatively mature, it is unlikely that radical new parsing algorithms will be able to make overwhelming improvements over the existing methods. An interesting departure from the syntactic-based approach is that of Roger Schank, a Yale researcher and entrepreneur who developed a technique that relies only lightly on syntax and very heavily on semantics. One syntactic approach that holds promise is that developed by Mitch Marcus in his Ph.D. thesis at MIT. Marcus described a "wait-and-see" parser that eliminates the redundant work done by many context-free and ATN parsers. It achieves this by delaying the decision of what role a particular phrase plays in a sentence. This is particularly useful in dealing with ambiguous phrases, which are the most difficult problem faced by syntactic analyzers.

Roughly speaking there are two types of ambiguity commonly encountered: lexical ambiguity, arising from words having more than one meaning; and structural ambiguity, arising from different legal syntactic arrangements of the same words. Because of ambiguity, many sentences can be legally parsed in several ways, and each legal sequence of rules would generate a different parse tree. Lexical ambiguity might permit more than one arc to be allowed because a word such as "hit" may legally play the role of a verb or a noun. Structural ambiguity might arise because more than one option may be legal within the context-free rules themselves. For example, when two prepositional phrases follow a noun, they may be nested (as in the example in Figure 3.3) or both prepositional phrases may modify the lead noun.

It is absolutely essential that a parser intended for commercial use be capable of dealing with these and other forms of ambiguity. Many parsers stop after finding a single correct parse, even if multiple parses are possible. Worse yet, some ignore ambiguities altogether by allowing words to be defined with only one meaning, or by using a very restricted grammar. Such approaches are certain to disappoint users because the richness of the English language is such that ambiguity arises with surprising frequency, even in simple applications. It is critical that a true natural language system deal with ambiguity efficiently and effectively.

Semantics—Shades of Meaning

Semantics refers to meaning. It is difficult at the outset to even think of how a computer could represent meaning at all, much less the meaning of a particular sentence. Before describing different ways of representing meaning on a computer, it is important to understand the difference between syntax and semantics. The simple phrase "a hot cup of coffee" illustrates the distinction. A syntactic parse of the phrase would indicate that the word "hot" modifies the word "cup." But we know that the true meaning of the phrase is that the coffee is hot, but not necessarily the cup. No matter what semantic representation we choose, it is clear that it will differ from the parse tree, in terms of where the word "hot" is attached.

There are virtually as many semantic representations as there are natural language systems. The semantic representation is almost always linked closely to the domain in which the system is to be applied. This is because no single scheme for dealing with meaning has been found that works equally well across a variety of applications. For this reason, it is necessary to customize a representation that is best for the task at hand.

If the task is a logical question-answering system, the semantic representation might be based on the predicate calculus to aid in theorem proving. If the task is database query, the semantic representation might be based on a relational calculus similar to that of a relational database management system. For other applications a hierarchical taxonomy is appropriate. In any case, the structure built to represent the meaning of a sentence must be consistent with the scheme used to represent the information stored in the system's knowledge base. This is because the knowledge base must be referred to in attempting to understand the meaning of a new sentence. (How else would you know that coffee should be hot, not the cup?) It must also allow the new sentence to ultimately add to the knowledge base if it represents a new fact. Therefore, the representations employed to discern a sentence's meaning must be compatible with, if not identical to, the representation of information in the computer's knowledge base.

No matter what representation is used, the procedure for building the semantic structure proceeds as follows. Initially, there is a definition for each word in the sentence. Each word definition is a mini-semantic structure. The individual meanings are combined according to how the parse tree indicates they syntactically relate to one another. When one word modifies another its semantic structure alters the semantic structure of the other word. The mini-semantic structures are merged first word-by-word, then phrase-by-phrase, and ultimately clause-by-clause. As more and more words participate in the structure the more complete it becomes. Eventually the structure that represents the meaning of the entire sentence is generated.

Although this description indicates that semantic analysis follows syntactic analysis, it is almost essential for the two to take place simultaneously on a computer. As the parse tree is being constructed, the corresponding semantic structure is built. This allows the semantic knowledge to affect the syntactic analysis. Often semantic information will help rule out certain interpretations that would be syntactically correct, but meaningless. This is critical in reducing the number of interpretations that must be considered and diminishing the number of dead ends reached by the machine.

Pragmatics—Determining Intent

Pragmatics refers to those aspects of natural language discourse that are not explicitly contained in the words actually used. Much communication takes place, not by what was actually said, but by what was intended. As such, pragmatics must often rely upon a broad range of knowledge about the world to recognize how the context of a sentence can alter its meaning.

Pragmatic analysis usually takes place after semantic analysis is complete, when the meaning of the sentence is being merged into the context of the ongoing dialog or the knowledge base. Often this merging process will indicate that some processing other than the normal is required. For example, in a database query context, there can be questions such as "WHO IS SMITH?" or "WHAT IS THE SALARY OF SMITH AND JONES?" If the normal response to a "who" question is to print the person's name, such a response is clearly inappropriate for a question such as "WHO IS SMITH?" since the user already knows Smith's name. Similarly printing only the two salaries in response to the second query would be inappropriate since the user would not be able to associate a salary to either Smith or Jones. In such a case, pragmatics dictate answering with what the user wants, not simply giving precisely what was asked for.

Another example in the context of a mechanical repair dialog is a question such as "WHERE IS THE WRENCH?" In such a case the system must determine why the user is looking for a wrench, and if such a step is inappropriate at this particular time in the repair process, then the system may not want to answer the question at all. Instead, it should indicate to the user where he should be in the repair process and indicate the next step.

Pragmatic analysis is always very application dependent, but it can frequently play a role in clarifying interpretations, because pragmatics often indicate how far out-of-context a particular request may be. It is usually desirable to prefer interpretations that are in closest context with the ongoing dialog. While pragmatic analysis is an important aspect of making a natural language system act intelligently, it is also the most difficult of the analysis functions to achieve. People are good at pragmatics because they have extensive world knowledge and can easily place statements in the proper context. Computers, which by necessity contain only knowledge about specific domains, often lack the broad view necessary to properly catch the intent of a sentence. This skill will improve only gradually as computers are programmed with more and more knowledge about the world.

Level of Semantic Primitives

One of the most critical decisions that must be made during the creation of any commercial natural language system is the level of semantic primitives that are to be used. The semantic primitives represent the lowest-level detailed knowledge that the system can understand. With more detailed semantic primitives, finer distinctions can be made in the definitions of words, allowing more precise representations of the meaning. The only drawback to using such low-level detailed semantic primitives is that all definitions must ultimately be made in terms of these primitives, an extremely labor-intensive process. In general, the lower the level of semantic primitives being used the more definitions that must be made overall and the more intricate the process required for each definition.

This is one of the most difficult tradeoffs that must be made in the design of a commercial natural language system. In order to be commercially viable a system must make it easy for its users to add and change definitions in the computer's dictionary, or "lexicon." This argues for a relatively high level (less detailed) of semantic primitives to simplify the definition process as much as possible. However, if the semantic primitives are not detailed enough, the system will be unable to make certain important distinctions.

Fortunately, in most commercial applications the level of detail required by the application is limited by other components of the application. For example, in a database query application, it is pointless for the natural language system's semantics to be more precise than the level of semantics represented in the database itself. To go beyond this level only increases the difficulty of making definitions, without any benefit. It is important to take advantage of these inherent restrictions when they exist.

Many attempts at building commercial natural language systems have failed because they tried to use semantic primitives that were too detailed. This results in systems that can only be adapted to new applications by the original designers, since the definitional scheme is too complex for the user organization to understand and modify. Another manifestation of this problem is a requirement that the existing data on a computer be reformatted in more detail for storage under a specialized data management system. This occurs when the decision is made to improve the semantic detail of the database rather than limit the representation of the natural language system. Needless to say, this choice severely limits the commercial viability of the resulting system, since few customers will choose to restructure their entire database, even if it means a slight improvement in linguistic fluency.

Solving the Entire Problem

The use of natural language technology today centers around its role as an interface between nontechnical users and the computer in business problem-solving environments. The user asks questions, phrased in ordinary English, and the natural language system is responsible for deriving the answer to the question. It turns out that natural language technology only plays a small part in the function of the overall system. In general, there are other major software systems involved, such as a database management system, a statistical tool, and a graphics facility. It is the responsibility of the natural language system to orchestrate all of these components to produce the answer for the user. For this reason pure natural language technology is a necessary, but not totally sufficient, component. It is also essential to have the ability to partition the work among the other software tools, to have interfaces to each of the popular subsystems, and to combine the results of each component into the final answer for the user.

Even within the realm of language analysis, there are a number of important capabilities that are requirements for commercial viability that many people do not associate with natural language analysis per se. It's good to think of the natural language interface as a specialized assistant that translates requests from the user to the formal languages the underlying subsystems require. As such, the natural language system must understand the user on his or her own terms, and must also deal with the formal computer systems as they are. Special problems arise from both of these requirements.

In terms of dealing with the user, two important issues arise. The first is the user's "conceptual view," which refers to the way in which the user thinks about the data and the implicit assumptions made in referring to it. The second is ambiguity, which arises not because the user is trying to be oblique, but because he or she is concentrating on the business problem at hand and isn't always aware that a request may have more than one possible interpretation.

On the computer system's side, two other important issues arise from the fact that the structure of today's corporate databases can be very complex. In order to insulate the user from this complexity, the natural language system must be capable of dealing with such issues as time-series aggregations of data, and a variety of summarization levels within the data. Each of these four issues warrants a closer look.

Conceptual View

It is helpful to think of three very different views of computerized information as shown in Figure 3.4. The "physical view" is the way the data is stored in the computer, that is, where each individual fact is actually stored. This low-level perspective is too detailed for anything but a computer to deal with.

Programmers actually interact with the data in a somewhat higher level with what is commonly referred to as the "logical view." This level organizes the information into a set of files that store very precisely defined pieces of information. The user's "conceptual view" is the way that the user thinks of the data. It is extremely important to realize that

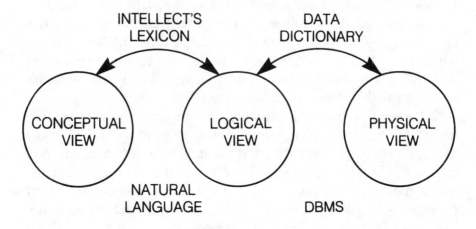

Figure 3.4 Intellect's Lexicon Defines the Mapping Between the User's Conceptual view and the Database Management System's (DBMS's) Logical View.

the user's conceptual view can be very different from the programmer's logical view, because there are a variety of possible logical views for any conceptual view. From the user's perspective, it shouldn't matter how the data is physically or logically structured on the computer. The user's questions make sense, and should be answered in the same way, no matter what the logical database design happens to be.

In essence, the role of the natural language interface is to translate between the conceptual view and the logical view. The degree to which the system supports the user's conceptual view is the degree to which the system will provide real value to the user. It is common for natural language systems that have not been subject to heavy commercial use to force the user to understand the logical view. These systems are ultimately found unacceptable by the market because they require the user to know certain facts that most don't know, and don't want to learn. Since the role of a natural language interface is to translate between the conceptual view and the logical view, any natural language system that forces the user to understand the logical view is failing to address the very problem that it was created to solve.

The solution of this problem involves the use of a lexicon, which defines both the way the user employs words in the conceptual sense, and how the words are represented in the logical database design. This lexicon can be created and maintained by the user once certain linkages are established to the underlying logical view. The leverage obtained through the proper use of the lexicon is substantial. By making a finite number of definitions in the lexicon the user can actually employ an infinite number of English phrasings to analyze the data. This is because English grammar allows the words defined in the lexicon to be used in so many different orders. There is no need for the user to predefine the meaning of sequences of words or entire requests, only individual words need be defined.

Ambiguity

Ambiguity is the biggest single factor that separates natural language from any of the formal computer languages. As noted, English is ambiguous, with almost all words having more than one meaning. In addition, the structure of the English language allows some uncertainty as to which words are being modified by a particular word or phrase. On the other hand, all formal computer languages are designed in such a way that there can be no ambiguity. Words have one and only one meaning, and the language only allows one interpretation from a given sequence of words.

At first blush ambiguity appears to be an annoyance that natural language systems are forced to deal with, but that formal languages are spared. Actually, ambiguity is a blessing in disguise. Just because the formal languages eliminate ambiguity from their specifications, there's no guarantee that the ambiguity has also been eliminated from the mind of the user. That is, just because the formal system's documentation insists that a word has one and only one meaning doesn't mean that people will always use it that way. What it does ensure is that if a user inadvertently employs the word in the wrong way, then the formal system will simply misinterpret the request. No warning. No error message. Just wrong answers. All because the formal system assumes that the user is abiding by all of its rules and regulations, and using words only the one way it uses them.

Because of the ambiguity inherent in English, a natural language system is forced to consider a variety of meanings that could have been intended by the user. In some cases the system must go back to the user and ask for clarification. This is why ambiguity is a blessing in disguise. The natural language system must create an atmosphere in which the system is looking out for the user. A natural language system cannot afford to assume that the user knows all the rules. As such it provides a safety net that warns the user when the possibility of other interpretations arises.

One of the most important aspects of evaluating natural language systems is how effectively they deal with ambiguity. The lexicon should be capable of storing many different meanings for each word. The grammar must allow multiple interpretations to be considered in certain circumstances. Without these facilities it is impossible to provide a very secure safety net.

Aggregates

Many business problems involve tracking performance against plan or comparing performance with the same period last year. For this reason many corporate databases contain not only the current status of the situation, but also what the status was in the past, what status was planned for, and what the status should be in the future. These types of databases, although extremely common, are notably hard to use with formal languages because the user's conceptual view is radically different from the database's logical design.

An example helps illustrate this point. Assume that the brand manager for a company wants to track the firm's sales volume in both dollars and units sold. The brand manager would want sales for last year, this year, and projections for next year in the database. For analytical purposes the sales for each month and each quarter as well as year-to-date sales would be required. For the past year and the current year, the database must contain both actual and estimated sales. Essentially, the user would like to get answers to questions such as:

"COMPARE THE ACTUAL SALES OF COPIERS LAST MONTH TO THE ESTIMATES."

"SHOW ME A PIE CHART OF THE YTD SALES IN EACH REGION."

"COMPARE THIS YEAR'S SALES TO LAST YEAR'S, FOR EACH PRODUCT."

Obviously, such a database and the ability to query it in English would be extremely useful in tracking performance. It all seems very reasonable and straightforward from the business perspective.

However, the logical design of such a database is quite complicated. What we have described requires storing over 150 sales statistics (3 years, 16 time periods, both actual and estimated data, for both sales units and dollars). The database considers each of these 150 data items, with category names like 86-ACT-YTD-SALES or 87-EST-FEB-UNITS, to be the appropriate level of detail for the user. But, as we can see from the sample questions above, the user thinks in terms of concepts such as "actual," "this year," or "year to date." There is rarely a reference to a data item that is fully qualified by all four components of the name. In fact, in the examples above we can see how natural it is for the user to factor out common components of the analysis. For example, in a phrase such as "actual and estimated ytd sales" the ytd and sales terms have been factored out. The meaning is to apply them both to the actual and estimated terms.

Experience has shown that forcing users to perform the translation from the conceptual way they think about the data to the fully qualified category names is unacceptable to the bulk of the user community. It is painful to be forced to be fully specific each time you want to refer to the data. For example, users expect that the computer should have the common sense to know that a reference to a time period in the future is obviously a reference to an estimated data. To be forced to be so precise takes the user's mind off the business problem at hand.

Other approaches for data access have been tried, such as providing the users with a list of options, or "menu," from which to choose. But even for the relatively simple times-series application, this approach would require the user to select the right name from a menu of 150 names that all look very much alike. And this selection process would have to be performed each time the user wanted to refer to a data item.

This example illustrates the gap that can exist between the user's conceptualization of the data and how it is actually stored. As such, it shows the attractive simplicity of just letting the user express himself in his own terms. By automating the translation from the conceptual view to the logical view the user is allowed to continue business problem-solving without interruption or distraction. In addition, the translation is carried out more accurately and efficiently than it would be by untrained users attempting to make requests in formal computer languages.

Summarization

Actually, the situation is much worse than described in the previous section because of another very common feature of corporate databases. The brand manager using the database described in the last section would likely be performing analysis of the sales in different markets, through different channels of distribution, and for several products within a product line. For example, if sales were off for a particular product, it would be important to know if it was just in certain markets where new competition was being encountered, or whether the downturn was due to the failure of a particular distributor to meet plan. Once again these are very reasonable business problems that translate into a very complex database design.

The issue at work here is based on the fact that the brand manager is rarely interested in the detailed facts of the sale of a particular product in a particular market through a particular distribution channel. Normally the brand manager's analysis is at a much more global level in which the individual transactions have been summarized. Thus, if presented with a database that contains only detailed information, each question asked by the brand manager would have to include specific instructions on how to appropriately summarize the data. Once again we discover that brand managers don't think this way. When they ask for information such as "WHAT ARE THE TOP 5 MARKETS FOR WORD PROCESSORS?", it is implicit to them that they mean the sales summarized for all channels and for all products within the word processor product line. Again, to force them to explicitly ask for this information in each request is to force them to take their minds off the business problems they are trying to solve. This is properly part of the mapping from the conceptual view to the logical view that should be performed for the user by the natural language system.

There are two additional important points with regard to the summarization of data. First, consider what would happen in a formal language environment in which the user must explicitly ask for summarization. If the user makes an error and leaves out the summarization along one dimension, or puts in summarization along an extra dimension, what happens? No error messages. No warnings. Just wrong answers! Omissions such as these are of a semantic nature. Leaving out a summarization level is syntactically correct. Therefore, no formal system can detect this type of mistake. Worse yet, the format of the answer looks correct since it is likely to be a partially summarized result. In this environment it is highly likely that the user will simply be misinformed without warning.

The second issue is that of efficiency. By embedding precomputed subtotals within the database, enormous efficiencies can be achieved because questions can be answered by reading only small portions of the file rather than reading all of it. This technique is so important that it is used in virtually all commercial databases of this type. But it puts a further burden on the users if they must access the summarized information through a formal-language system. Now, in addition to everything else, the user is forced to consider whether the summary level already exists or not. If it does, the user must ask the question one way. If it does not, then the user must ask the question another way. It is likely that the particular syntax will even be a function of whether the summary data is indexed or not. It should come as no surprise that users are confused by all of this.

This is another area where a good natural language system really pays off. By automating this process as part of the conceptual to logical mapping, the user is assured that the proper level of summarization will automatically be computed and that it will be done in the most efficient method possible.

Data-Analysis Capability

It is a rare business problem that is solved by dumping raw data into the hands of the user. Usually that data has to be summarized or statistically analyzed before it can be applied to a real business situation. Many people immediately jump to the conclusion that this means putting heavy-handed statistical tools, such as multiple linear regression or Box-Jenkins Analysis, in the hands of the user. In fact, only a few simple statistical tools such as minimum, maximum, average, totals, and comparisons are usually needed. Computational problems arise not because of the complexity of the statistical tool, but because of the requirement to use several simple tools within one request.

The issue is really the manner in which the user chooses to specify how the output of one function is to become the input of another. For example, consider the request "I WONDER HOW THE AVERAGE SALARY OF WOMEN COMPARES TO THAT OF MEN?" This request requires first the calculation of the average salary of both men and women, and then these numbers must be compared to each other. It's clearly not an issue of complex statistical analysis, but many formal languages require intricate procedures to pass the results of one calculation to another. Often multiple levels of "nested" parentheses are required. In more complex cases the user would be forced to open a temporary file to store the intermediate results and then read the results in later. All of this begins to force the user into a programmer's mindset of breaking up the problem into a sequence of steps that can be expressed to the machine.

A good natural language system solves this problem by first determining what statistical functions are required to answer the problem. Then it determines what additional steps are required to solve or speed up the solution of the problem. For instance, in the previous example the system would know to continue sorting the data by sex before computing the averages to speed the computation. Finally, the system orchestrates the invocation of the various statistical functions and the passing of data between them. This is another critical function that is being performed for the user. Without it, the user is forced to worry about any number of detailed issues that are not relevant to the business problem. Needless to say, any error made by the user in this process will lead to either frustration or wrong answers. The value added by the natural language facility in this regard is quite substantial, and goes far beyond merely translating English statements into machine-readable code.

Speech

Before concluding our discussion of natural languages, it is important to examine the relationship between natural language and speech-recognition technology. It is apparent to everyone who read science fiction that we are destined to interact with computers by the spoken word, just as we interact with each other. But getting computers to recognize speech is a difficult AI problem in its own right. Recent progress toward that goal has already made certain commercial applications feasible. Of particular interest is the symbiotic relationship between speech-understanding technology and natural language processing. Speech recognition needs natural language to realize its full potential, and natural language needs speech recognition to separate it from various alternative technologies.

The markets for speech technology can be roughly broken into three segments: single word, sentences without meaning, and sentences with meaning. The single-word applications are fixed tasks where only a small number of alternatives are possible, such as selecting choices from a screen menu. Single-word applications have been in use for some time without generating much excitement in the marketplace. The latest voice-recognition systems have sufficiently larger vocabularies than their predecessors to actually permit users to speak full sentences to the computer.

In some full-sentence speech systems it is not necessary for the system to make an attempt to understand the meaning of the words being spoken. An example of this is the much-talked-about "voice-activated typewriter." In theory, such a machine could eliminate the need for secretary typists, since executives could dictate their own letters directly into the computer. Of course, secretaries do more than simply type when creating a document, and until voice-typewriters are priced competitively with word processors, they may experience only limited success.

The most exciting uses of voice technology are applications where the user speaks in full sentences to convey a thought to the machine. This obviously requires natural language processing capability to figure out the meaning of the sentences. Therefore it will be through the combined use of voice and natural language technologies that we will begin to approach the applications depicted in science-fiction movies.

In this sense, voice requires natural language to achieve its full potential. A similar analysis shows how natural language benefits from voice. In today's marketplace there are several alternative methods of giving users access to computer-based information. These involve menu systems, fourth-generation languages, and spreadsheets, as well as natural language systems. The only one of these approaches substantially enhanced through the use of voice technology is natural language. In this sense, natural language needs voice to distance itself from the alternative technologies. There is no question that voice recognition combined with natural language processing will open computer access to a whole new class of users.

4

Expert Systems

- Decision Trees
- Knowledge Bases
- Knowledge-Base Query
- Simulating Human Problem Solving
- From Inferencing to Intelligent Behavior
- Knowledge-Based Systems
- Choosing the Problem

Natural language constitutes a popular goal of AI developers largely because, more than anything else, it represents a fundamental characteristic that signifies the unique intelligence of human beings. Expert systems instill awe for a different reason. These systems contain the knowledge and the means to process it known to only a few select people. So, while natural language represents the innate talent of the masses, expert systems embody the rarified knowledge accumulated by some of the most talented people.

Consequently, expert systems tend to generate more interest than natural language systems. After all, virtually everyone is an expert user of natural language, whereas few of us can expect to surpass the knowledge contained in an expert system that diagnoses medical ailments or analyzes a chemical compound's spectrographic data.

Since, as their name implies, expert systems codify and exploit the knowledge of human experts, it would seem that such systems are inherently more complex and advanced than the systems that tackle the problem of natural language understanding. In fact, the reverse is probably true. This apparent contradiction has been addressed by Marvin Minsky of MIT, who notes that expert systems have only shown success in performing adult-level chores, such as the playing of Master-level chess. "Isn't it odd, when you think about it, how even the earliest AI programs excelled at 'advanced' subjects yet had no common sense?" he wrote in *Technology Review* (November/December 1983, p. 80). "Why could we make programs do grown-up things before we could make them do childish things? The answer is a somewhat unexpected paradox: much 'expert' adult thinking is basically much simpler than what happens in a child's ordinary play." Minsky goes on to note that, "An expert can sometimes get by with deep, but narrow, bodies of knowledge—but common sense is, technically, a lot more complicated."

Natural language understanding is not the only superficially simple task that actually proves to be very processing intensive. Early workers in robotics encountered difficulty in getting a robot to open a door. The robot could find the door's handle, grasp it without crushing it, and then turn it the appropriate amount. But then it would pull the door off its hinges. Without a great deal of calculation about the circular-arc trajectory of a door on its hinges, the robot would attempt to pull the handle along a straight line, with disastrous results.

Of course, even young children can open doors successfully without any knowledge of the physics involved in the process. They can do this because they have a wonderful capacity of give and take. When they pull on door handles and feel them moving away from a straight-line track, they subconsciously let their hands follow the same motion. Unfortunately, it's very difficult to program a computer to "go with the flow."

It would be a mistake to infer from the above observations that all adult-level processes are somehow more amenable to AI solutions than problems routinely solved by children. If we stay within the same dimension of problem-solving, in fact, the adult-level functions will typically far surpass those of a child. Take language understanding. It's clear that adult communications, with the increased use of cues such as spoken inflections and body language, are much more subtle and complex than the communication between children. It usually turns out that age is a poor metric to apply in evaluating the appropriateness of AI for solving a certain type of problem. What is really important is to identify problems that exist in narrowly defined environments in which the rules are precisely known. In theory, and to a degree in practice, expert systems are able to capitalize on these fundamental requirements.

Decision Trees

In order to grasp the basic notions behind expert systems, it is helpful to examine the classical technique that most closely resembles the expert-system process. This technique is known as "decision trees," and is commonly used in the process of identification or classification. Figure 4.1 shows a decision tree for identifying animals from some of their characteristics. The decision tree consists of a sequence of questions, each one of which narrows the number of possibilities. Ultimately only one animal meets all the conditions.

Obviously, a great deal of consideration must be given to the order in which the questions are asked. Furthermore, the complexity of the problem must be such that this stepwise reduction of the potential solutions is possible.

Decision trees are actually an example of a degenerate expert system, the simplest possible case. They exhibit the same "if-then" rules and uniform reduction in the search space of possible outcomes until only one conclusion remains. In fact, one can think of the process of defining a decision tree as very analogous to the process of building an expert system. The key issues are determining which questions to ask.

If you imagine the process of working with a biologist to define the decision tree of Figure 4.1, you will get a feel for the process of working with an expert to build an expert system. The knowledge is in the expert's head, but almost certainly not stored in the form of a decision tree. Through successive interactions with the biologist, and through many trial-and-error attempts at identifying a variety of animals with the evolving decision tree, the workable decision tree slowly takes shape over time.

The advantage of expert systems over decision trees is that the former are not restricted to the single-thread, top-down approach of the latter. Figure 4.2 shows the rule base that would correspond to the decision tree in Figure 4.1. In a sense, an expert system can be thought of as consisting of multiple decision trees, each attempting to solve the problem on its own. However, the answers to questions in one tree may affect which of the other trees are used. The goal is to provide

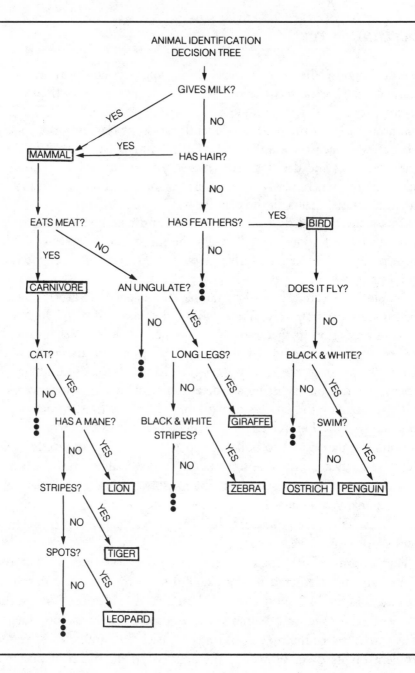

Figure 4.1   Decision Tree

Animal Identification Rule Base

If gives milk
then mammal

If has hair
then mammal

If has feathers
then bird

If eats meat
then carnivore

If bird
& does not fly
& black & white
& swims
then penguin

If bird
& does not fly
& black & white
& does not swim
then ostrich

If ungulate
& long legs
then giraffe

If ungulate
& does not have long legs
& black & white stripes
then zebra

If carnivore
& cat
& mane
then lion

If carnivore
& cat
& stripes
then tiger

If carnivore
& cat
& spots
then leopard

(A more complete expert system for Animal Identification appears in *ARTIFICIAL INTELLIGENCE*, by Patrick Winston, Addison Wesley.)

Figure 4.2   Rule Base Corresponding to Figure 4.1 Decision Tree

the rules without performing all the rigorous ordering required by a decision tree, and to somehow have the inference engine, figure out the right order to ask the questions (that is, use the rules).

There is one further advantage to this relationship between decision trees and expert systems. It may represent the best way of determining whether a particular problem is a good candidate for solution by the current level of expert-system technology. One might describe the capabilities of today's expert systems as being just beyond that of decision trees. In other words, if the problem is just outside the reach of straightforward decision trees, it is probably a good candidate for an expert system. Of course, if the problem can be solved by a decision tree, it should be, since the resulting solution can be inexpensively represented on paper and easily done by hand. If it is inconceivable that even a series of decision trees could solve a problem, then the problem may not prove to be amenable to solution by an expert system.

Some of the most successful industrial expert systems are for applications that previously made use of decision trees; and in these cases it is quite common to use the decision trees to help build the rule base. In fact, it is often possible to estimate the complexity of the required expert system by looking at the decision trees that may already exist in the problem area. If the applications are chosen well, the expert systems will be much more potent and more usable than the decision trees were.

Knowledge Bases

Before getting too far into a discussion of expert systems, it's useful to clarify the definition of the term "knowledge base." One caveat: this term should not be interpreted to mean "knowledge" in the same sense as "wisdom." A knowledge base consists of the first two components of rule-based programming: the unstructured set of facts, and inference rules for determining new facts. The primary distinction between knowledge bases and the more conventional "databases" is that the databases have a predetermined structure, while knowledge bases consist of a set of unstructured, almost isolated facts. The paths by which the facts are related in a knowledge base are determined "on the fly" as needed to solve a particular problem. The relationship between data items in conventional databases, by contrast, are designed into the database in advance. Another critical distinction between the two is that databases store all of their information explicitly, whereas the bulk of the information in a knowledge base is inferred from the basic facts using the inference rules.

A simple example will illustrate the point. Figure 4.3 represents the family relationships among a group of relatives. We all understand these simple family relationships, but they turn out to be hard to represent on a computer in a traditional database. However, it is very easy to represent them in a knowledge base. Our example will make use of the following family relationships:

PARENT	MOTHER	FATHER
SPOUSE	HUSBAND	WIFE
SIBLING	SON	DAUGHTER
UNCLE	AUNT	COUSIN

Figure 4.3   Family Relationships

In addition to these familial relationships, assume that data about each person's age and sex is stored as well as whether the individuals ever held political office and, if so, which office. These personal attributes aren't difficult to represent in a knowledge base or a database, but, as described later, storing the familial linkages in a conventional database is no easy task.

The first components of the knowledge base are the basic facts. These are stored in predicate form, that is, with the name of the relationship first, followed by the names of the people in a prescribed order. To store the fact that "Joseph is the father of Jack" we write (FATHER JOSEPH JACK). To enter the fact that "Jack is the brother of Bobby" we write (BROTHER JACK BOBBY). We build the knowledge base by simply entering the basic facts.

There is no need to be complete. There is no need to store the same amount of information, or even the same type of information, for each person. The basic facts for our example might be as follows:

```
(FATHER JOSEPH JACK)
(HELD-OFFICE JACK PRESIDENT)
(BROTHER JACK BOBBY)
(BROTHER BOBBY TED)
(HELD-OFFICE TED SENATOR)
(WIFE JACKIE JACK)
(MOTHER JACKIE CAROLINE)
(MALE JACK)
(FEMALE CAROLINE)
```

The second components of the knowledge base are the inference rules. These are if-then rules that allow new facts to be created from the basic facts. These rules make use of variables such as X, Y, and Z, which will represent specific people when the inference rule is applied. For example, the simple inference rule, IF (HUSBAND X Y) THEN (WIFE Y X) represents the simple fact that if X is the husband of Y, then it is also true that Y is the wife of X. This obvious statement may seem unimportant, but it eliminates the need to enter the basic facts in a uniform way. We need not be concerned whether we have entered all facts regarding spouses with the HUSBAND or WIFE relationship. We could do it either way we like, even differently for different people. The inference rules can automatically determine the fact in whatever form we need.

Our sample knowledge base might contain the following inference rules:

```
IF (HUSBAND X Y) THEN (WIFE Y X)
IF (AND (PARENT X Y) (MALE X)) THEN (FATHER X Y)
IF (AND (BROTHER X Y) (BROTHER Y Z)) THEN (BROTHER
   X Z)
IF (BROTHER X Y) THEN (BROTHER Y X)
```

IF (AND (FATHER X Y) (BROTHER X Z)) THEN (UNCLE Z Y)
IF (AND (OR (UNCLE X Y) (AUNT X Y)) (SIBLING Z X))
    THEN (COUSIN Y Z)

If we were to try to represent this information in a traditional database, we must decide in advance exactly what information we want to store about each person, and how we want to store it (see Figure 4.4). It is hard to simultaneously represent PARENT, MOTHER, and FATHER, so we might be tempted to actually store only one and always access the data in that way. It would be much harder to derive the other two attributes once this choice was made. Also, it would be hard to add new relationships such as NEPHEW and NIECE if they weren't considered in the original design of the database.

ID	First Last Name		Sex	Spouse ID	1st Child	Next Sibling	Office Held
1	Joseph	Kennedy	M				
2	Jack	Kennedy	M	5	6	3	President
3	Bobby	Kennedy	M			4	
4	Ted	Kennedy	M				Senator
5	Jackie	Kennedy	F				
6	Caroline	Kennedy	F				

Figure 4.4   Traditional Database for Family Relationships

Thus, databases are considerably more rigid than knowledge bases. Their structure requires a prior uniform definition for each entity and explicit storage of all facts. Once this design of the database is completed, it can be very difficult to change. Knowledge bases, on the other hand, represent the data in a much more dynamic fashion. Not only can the facts change, but the structure and the interrelationships among the facts can change as the knowledge base is being used.

Knowledge-Base Query

Querying the knowledge base is the analog of querying a database. We have seen examples of fourth-generation language queries that specify the selection criteria and attributes of the data to be displayed in answer to the question. The database query processor retrieves all the records that satisfy the selection criteria and prints the requested attributes of those records. A query to probe a knowledge base is very similar. In its simplest form it specifies a selection condition or predicate. The knowledge base query processor determines all the "atoms" (people in our example) for which the selection predicate is true. A simple example will illustrate the analogy. Suppose we wanted to list all the women. A formal database query might be:

PRINT NAME
FROM PEOPLE-FILE
WHERE SEX = 'F'.

The corresponding knowledge base query would be:

(LIST X (FEMALE X))

This knowledge-base query would be read as "List all X such that X is female."

Since these queries involve the retrieval of explicitly stored information, there isn't a significant difference between them. Let's now formulate a simple request for information not explicitly stored. Suppose we wanted to know the names of Caroline's uncles. (LIST X (UNCLE X CAROLINE)) would do it. This request would cause the query interpreter to search the knowledge base for people that it could prove were the uncle of Caroline. It could either be explicitly stored or inferred from one of the rules. A database query for this request is much more intricate because databases are much less adept at representing relationships between records than they are at explicitly storing attributes about each record. For this reason the concept of UNCLE is much harder to represent in a database than SEX. It follows that if a concept is hard to represent, it is also hard to formulate a query to extract it.

A more complex problem would be to find the men in this family who might soon be ready to seek political office. We might ask for the sons and nephews of anyone who has held political office (LIST X (ALL Y (AND (OR (SON X Y) (NEPHEW X Y)) HELD-OFFICE Y))).

This example is particularly interesting because it makes use of a new concept, that of NEPHEW. In a database environment such a query would simply fail. The concept of nephew would have to be defined to the system before such a request could be answered. As stated earlier, this type of relationship would be hard to define in a traditional database. In a knowledge base the system could interrupt processing of the query and ask for an inference rule to define NEPHEW. This could be done by adding:

IF (UNCLE X Y) THEN (NEPHEW Y X)

With this rule added to the knowledge base, the system can proceed to answer the original question. This illustrates the robustness of knowledge-base systems in coping with unanticipated problems.

Simulating Human Problem Solving

As is evident from the preceding section, the key function of the knowledge-base system is to be able to prove things to be either true or false. When performing knowledge-base queries it applies the selection criteria to each atom and tries to determine if it is true. In order to do this the system works backwards from trying to prove the overall condition, first by looking to see if it is stored explicitly as a fact, and if not, by looking for a rule that would help prove all or part of the condition. Once such a rule is found the system begins to try to prove the IF portion of that rule. This "backward-chaining" inference process is very similar to the bottom-up parsing methods discussed in Chapter 3.

The terminology used in expert systems literature involves the use of logical terms to indicate this reverse flow of the logic. Rules are expressed in the form: IF <antecedent> THEN <consequent>. The antecedent condition may contain several conditions and the consequent may conclude several facts.

In a fashion similar to the backward-chaining inference mechanism, "forward chaining" works from the given information to the goal. This approach is very similar to the process used to perform high-school geometry proofs. Still, even though all proofs are presented in a forward-chaining manner (from given information to conclusion), the process of figuring out the problem is often done by working backward from the goal. In practice, a mixture of both forward and backward chaining is the most effective method for problem solving. Not surprisingly, many expert system inference engines provide both a forward- and backward-chaining capability.

The inference engine that is the heart of an expert system maintains a list of all the assertions that must be proved true in order to make a conclusion regarding the overall problem. For each item on this list it first looks for the assertion stored as an explicit fact in the knowledge base. If not found, the inference engine searches the consequents of the rule base to find those that can help prove the assertion. For each such rule it will add the antecedents of that rule to the list of assertions yet to be proved. Once all of the antecedents of a rule have been proven true the consequents of that rule can be stored as facts. In particular, the consequent that caused us to select the rule in the first place can be removed from the assertion list. Once everything on the assertion list has been proven true, the overall problem has been solved.

In essence, the inference process is searching for the deduction chain that will prove the assertion made by the problem. This is equivalent to a parser searching for the derivation sequence that will prove that the syntax of a sentence is correct. The same efficiency issues arise in the knowledge-base search process with an important simplification. There is no analog of ambiguity in the knowledge base since there is no need to prove the statement true in more than one way. The first deductive sequence found is sufficient, and there is no need to look for other proofs as there is the need to look for multiple interpretations in the natural language context.

Still the issue of search efficiency is critical. The AI literature is full of sophisticated search strategies that try to adjust the order in which the rules are applied to find the solution as fast as possible. Since more than one rule can be used to prove a desired consequent, some basis for choosing which rule to employ first must be determined. Typically, this ordering is based on an estimate of how many steps are likely to remain after the given rule is applied. The rule with the lowest estimate is applied first. Any relevant knowledge in the knowledge base can be exploited in making the estimate. In this way the knowledge serves two functions. First, it is used to aid in the proof of each assertion. Second, it helps guide the process to the fastest possible solution. This double benefit is one of the key leverage points of building an accurate and extensive knowledge base.

From Inferencing to Intelligent Behavior

How does this simple inference process get turned into a simulation of expert-human problem solving? This question is no different from that which asks how the formal assignment statements, loops, and conditional statements of third-generation programming languages are used to produce packages that solve complex payroll or general ledger applications. The answer to both is that it lies in the hands of the programmer. By properly specifying the rules to allow a constant simplification of the problem until only basic facts are required, it is possible to solve some impressive problems. There are two specific techniques that are used in applying the rule-based technology to difficult problems: the ability to reason at different levels of abstraction, and the use of certainty factors.

We have already seen how the ATN parser performs analysis at different levels of detail. There are specific ATNs for the sentence level, the clause level, and the phrase level. One of the advantages of the ATN over pure context-free rules is the partitioning of the rule base that occurs with the former. To parse a prepositional phrase only a small number of rules need to be searched. This also serves to focus the construction of the rules to address a specific subproblem.

In a similar fashion it is important to break the solution of the knowledge-base problems into subproblems that can be addressed in isolation. For this reason a number of rule-based languages have facilities that allow the expression of solutions on several different levels of abstraction. In fact, some of the levels may be specified more conveniently in a procedural manner rather than in the fifth-generation rule-based fashion.

It is common to have at least two explicit levels of abstraction: a planning or strategic level, and a tactical level. The planning level attempts to organize the overall approach to the problem in terms of high-level constructs. The verification of the details is left to the tactical level. If the system is capable of generating a variety of plans to be tried, then a third "meta-planning" level may also exist to generate different plans. The nature of the problem solving on each of these levels may be quite different.

Another facility is the use of certainty-factor weightings on each of the rules. The weights estimate the likelihood of the consequent following from the condition. In a medical diagnosis application the least common diseases would have a lower certainty. By carrying the certainty factors throughout the analysis the system is capable of ranking the set of conclusions that are ultimately made.

Knowledge-Based Systems

There is another important dimension in which expert systems can be viewed. This perspective is based on the relative ratio of facts versus inference rules required to solve a particular problem. Typically, adding "expertise" to a system means adding more inference rules and increasing the complexity of interaction among the rules.

Today's rule-based technology is better at handling knowledge-based applications that have large fact bases, but relatively straightforward inference requirements. An application such as medical diagnosis obviously requires extensive expertise as well as an extensive collection of facts. Otherwise, young doctors with more recent exposure to a range of medical facts would uniformly be better physicians than old doctors. Rule-heavy applications such as medical diagnosis are particularly difficult because of the complex interactions that can take place during a diagnosis. For example, it is not uncommon in medical cases for a patient to be suffering from more than one malady. In some instances, the original problem may cause secondary problems, whose manifestations are the primary cause of the patient's complaints. In such situations it is pointless to address the secondary problem without also discovering and curing the original ailment. Since these interactions are often missed by human doctors, it should come as no surprise that they can push today's expert system technology beyond its limits. Fortunately there are many situations in which multiple problems occur either infrequently, or only in certain common combinations. In such cases, workable expert systems can be built to address these applications.

Fact-intensive applications, on the other hand, are solved more by having the right information at the right time than by extensive expertise or experience. That is, the criteria for a fact-intensive expert system is partly that the program deals with a problem that can be largely solved through an organized structuring of the knowledge base. Also, a rapidly changing environment can create a situation in which simply having the ability to quickly assess a body of knowledge can solve the problem. An example of this might be a fact-intensive program that monitors a nuclear reactor.

In a sense, fact-intensive problems are inherently simpler than those that depend on extensive and complex sets of rules. Often there is more than one valid solution to the problem. In such cases, one of the advantages of an automated solution is simply that it yields a consistent solution each time it is given the same input. Such is not the case when humans do the task.

After we have had the experience of solving a number of fact-intensive problems we can possibly leverage that experience and begin to address problems with a higher requirement for sophisticated inferencing. The difference between the two types of systems is not a clear line, but a continuum of increasingly difficult problems. Given the current state of the technology, this makes the selection of the problem to be addressed one of the most critical decisions to be made.

Choosing the Problem

The good news is that the difficulty of solving AI problems has nothing to do with the financial reward for solving them. Although there will undoubtedly be financial rewards for solving many intensive problems, the rewards for addressing simpler fact intensive problems can be just as great. Therefore it is possible to reap the benefits to be had in developing straightforward knowledge-based systems while waiting for the technology to evolve before investing too heavily in solving extremely complex problems. This is a fortunate set of circumstances, since few developers have the ability or the financial might to tackle commercial development of complex expert systems. The very marketability of the simple knowledge-based products provides a relatively secure near-term niche within which developers can learn the AI ropes and possibly turn a profit at the same time. For consumers, this means that AI-based products will be more readily available than might otherwise have been the case.

Not only vendors of the technology, but many users are beginning to experiment with rule-based programming. In some industries such as oil, competitive pressures may even force the firms to invest in developing sophisticated expert systems just to ensure being in a position to capitalize on AI as soon as possible. For most companies, solving the knowledge-based problems will be ample experience for learning about the technology and positioning themselves for the future.

Some development managers have suggested that they start out by using the rule-based approach to solve some of their current programming problems, such as the payroll, before moving on to more exotic things. However, as noted earlier, there is no reason to believe that the rule-based approach would lead to any better solutions to the classic payroll problem.

As alluring as this perspective is, we've illustrated why, so far, it is false. The earlier programming methods have undeniable flaws; the interactions of their code can be so subtle that it may take days to track down a single program bug. But, while the fifth-generation methods may appear more straightforward, it's important to remember that they embody many of the characteristics of the other kinds of programming that make the analysis of a program's operation and the location of problems a very difficult procedure. The logical interactions in such rule-based programs can be extremely subtle, making any modification to the rule base an extremely delicate procedure.

What then are the clues that an application is an appropriate expert system problem that can effectively be addressed by the current rule-based technology? The answer to this question is the combination of two factors already discussed. The ideal application is heavily fact-based and the expertise is close to the decision-tree paradigm of stepwise reduction of the search space of possible solutions. In practice, it is hard to know exactly where any given application measures on this scale. But an important clue is to look at who is solving the problem now and at how much training and experience the people solving it require.

Of secondary importance is the status of the factual base that is required to solve the problem. Is it already available in machine-readable form? If not, what will be the cost of creating the knowledge base? Also of importance is the willingness of the user's staff to help create the factual base and inference rules, as well as their willingness to put the system into production when finished.

The choice of which application to start with is especially critical and, unless the user is sophisticated in the ways of rule-based programming, the decision should be made with expert consultation. This is a case where the selection of the wrong type of problem will almost certainly lead to failure. A wrong choice not only leads to the loss associated with failing to solve the target problem, but also incurs the opportunity costs of what the development resource could have produced on another project.

Despite the various limitations and risks inherent in today's expert-system/knowledge-based technology, the overall outlook for the field is bright. Considering that the first experimental expert systems appeared less than two decades ago, the technology has progressed at a rate equal to or faster than those of some other computer disciplines. As the following chapter indicates, the rule-based programming methodology is beginning to make its first strides into the commercial realm.

5

AI Products Emerge

- Inherent Difficulties
- Academic Mindset
- Technology-Driven Versus Market-Driven Technologies
- Expert-System Status
- Choosing a Product Niche
- Custom Development
- Knowledge-Engineering Tools
- Vertical Applications
- The Role of Business
- Societal Restrictions

We've seen how the artificial intelligence field relies upon powerful new programming methods, and how these methods can serve in the development of expert and natural language systems. Although these first steps into machine intelligence represent dramatic advances in the capabilities of computers, it's important to keep in perspective the relative weakness of present-day AI technology compared to human intelligence and senses. Indeed, if anything, the AI work lends dramatic proof to the natural tendency to view the mind as a tremendously complex entity. While AI researchers have managed to disentangle one or two threads from the web of intelligence, and have demonstrated their success by replicating on machines certain human characteristics, these efforts fall far short of solving the intricate riddles of how people think, create, and communicate.

Likewise, we must remember that as well-suited as rule-based programming is for solving AI tasks, it doesn't always lend itself to the development of lower-level applications. Since few applications will be solely in the realm of AI, many software programs will be hybrids that contain both traditional and rule-based portions. Because the need to use AI will vary from application to application, it's important to recognize that the package with the "most" AI will not necessarily be the "best" available product. The *value* of a product—its usefulness to a company or an individual—has no direct relationship to its AI content.

In fact, given the newness and the complexity of present-day AI programming, vendors looking to develop commercial application packages would be best off picking applications having the highest potential payoff while requiring the least amount of AI. Many AI developers seem to have the self-defeating tendency to devote all their resources to grappling with the most difficult, most interesting programming problems, without ever seriously considering the commercial worth of any solutions that might consequently emerge.

This is not to say that an effort should be made to avoid rule-based programming when circumstances clearly call for it. It's just that good marketing sense dictates that a developer's focus must first be on commercial viability and second on the best means to attain this viability. In some instances, AI will not be required at all; in others, it will be a critical element in a product's overall success. But even in the latter cases, care must be taken not to overestimate or to oversell the capabilities of artificial intelligence. What later generations of AI will someday make possible and what it can effect today are two very different things.

These limitations of present-day AI technology aren't, as many believe, because AI programs are so demanding of computer resources that they are impractical for all but the largest machines. A certain mythology has evolved that portrays AI products as resource hogs. It's for this reason, the theory goes, that AI hasn't spread rapidly to smaller machines such as personal computers. In fact, the slow pace of AI's appearance on small computers has more to do with the natural progression of program development common to any young programming environment.

It *is* true that the research and development phases of artificial intelligence are typically performed on large computers. As is the case with any type of program creation, it often makes sense to utilize whatever powerful tools are available during the development phase, even if the product is being designed to run on personal computers. With AI, where most developments are still breaking new ground, it pays to have fast computers and large memories to counterbalance the inefficiencies that inevitably result when doing something for the first time. However, it doesn't follow that just because AI developers may use powerful computers to create and test their programs that the completed programs will require similar-sized machines upon which to run.

Of all the artificial intelligence products, natural language systems were the first to the marketplace and have achieved the highest level of commercial use. Even for natural language systems, many companies have found it difficult to produce a product that is acceptable to users. Five years after the introduction of *Intellect*, the first commercial natural language system, there are still only a handful of competitive systems in evidence. A number of attempts have failed to reach the market; others that managed to enter the market fared badly upon their arrival. Similarly, the experience of companies bringing expert systems into the commercial realm has been checkered.

In essence, the problems arise for two main reasons: the inherent difficulty of solving AI problems, and the mindset and orientation of the individuals who have been trained in AI. These factors, combined with the lack of any real connection between academic computer science and commercial data processing, has made the commercialization of any AI technology a very slow process.

Inherent Difficulties

AI problems, by their very nature, do not have a crisp definition and cannot be totally solved. Bringing an AI product to market is a successive approximation of better and better solutions. It is not possible to produce a "perfect" natural language system, just as it is not possible to produce a "perfect" medical-diagnosis system. After all, even the human experts are not perfect.

In the end, all the AI developers can hope for is to cross over the line of commercial usefulness and viability, a line not well defined. Unlike other software products such as spreadsheets and word processors, for which the developers get to define their own rules, the solution to an AI problem must abide by the problem's natural rules. This makes it difficult to tell when the solution is complete enough. Going to market prematurely can be disastrous, but a common mistake is to continue trying to perfect the technology and never introduce a product at all.

For this reason, an attempt on the part of a company to produce an AI product is a substantial gamble. For non-AI software products it is a pretty safe bet that the investment of a technical resource will ultimately produce a marketable product. It is possible, indeed even likely, that the investment in an AI product may yield no return. This is particularly costly given that the AI development is likely to absorb a company's top development talent, a scarce resource that would almost certainly produce marketable results if applied in less risky traditional areas. These factors, combined with the fact that most software companies have their hands full extending their existing product lines, have kept most of the traditional software vendors out of the AI marketplace. It is an area where the "make versus buy" decision faced by these vendors clearly favors "buy."

For these reasons, most of the companies that have embarked on the road to the AI marketplace have been start-up firms founded by AI researchers interested in developing the fruits of their academic research. Reportedly more than $50 million has been invested in AI start-ups by the venture capital community during the past three years. Much of this has gone to researchers making their first stab in the commercial realm. These academics-turned-entrepreneurs generally have a solid grasp of the underlying AI technologies, but many have failed for an entirely different reason.

Academic Mindset

The mindset of the academic researcher newly turned entrepreneur is often very different from that of the successful software vendor. Along with the obvious changes faced when one moves from the academic to the commercial environment, there are some more subtle differences in orientation that make it hard for the academic to bring a product to market.

The most difficult challenge is to resist the temptation to pursue every interesting problem that pops up. As a researcher, one develops the instinct to seek out the interesting aspects of a problem. This ability is critical to the success of a researcher, but is deadly when employed by the product developer. The difficult aspects of bringing a product to market are more of the 90 percent perspiration variety, rather than the 10 percent inspiration. In the natural language arena, it's the exhaustive, and exhausting, testing of the hundreds of ways of phrasing very ordinary things. It is not the solution to some uniquely challenging syntactic construct. It is not the work that research papers are made of. Rather, it is all the detail work that turns a research prototype into a bulletproof product.

This development work, which entails improving the density of coverage rather than a breadth of coverage, typically takes from two to four years to complete. The reason for the long time period is because user feedback is an essential component in the process. It will typically take four or five attempts to detect the real problems encountered in the field, to respond to them, and to ultimately verify the solution. Given this, it is easy to see how the development period can stretch out.

The long development phase has killed AI start-ups for a couple of reasons. First, the researcher may lack the level of commitment to stick with the project for such an extended period. A person who has attained some stature in the academic world because of the quality and quantity of his or her research papers may not choose to work on nonpublishable work for such an extended period. This is particularly true for those individuals who have not been willing to completely cut their academic ties. The effort to produce an AI product requires such an enormously intensive effort and commitment that it almost certainly defies attempts at part-time solutions.

The extended developmental period puts additional financial pressures on AI start-ups since there is little likelihood of a quick payback. There are very few venture capitalists who would willingly wait four to five years before a product could be actively marketed. In some situations AI start-ups have prematurely gone public. If anything, this high profile puts additional pressure on the company to produce short-term gains. The result is a product brought to market prematurely. Inevitably, the market responds negatively, the company runs out of money, and it ends up in an extremely precarious financial position. This bleak scenario has been the fate of more than one AI start-up already.

Technology-Driven Versus Market-Driven Products

Another factor that makes it hard for academic researchers to develop a commercially viable product is that they are often too close to the technology. Customers don't buy a product because it contains a certain technology, they buy it because it solves a problem for them more cost effectively than other options. It is crucial, therefore, to first fully understand the nature of the customer's problem and then to develop the appropriate technology to effectively solve that problem.

In many cases AI researchers have merely taken the fruits of their academic research and tried to turn them into products. This "technology-driven" approach is the old story of having a solution that is looking for a problem to solve. In all too many cases, the particular approach taken by the researcher is not the most appropriate one to solve the customer's problem. It is a rare academician who will willingly retreat from the investment in and attachment to his own methodology, even though market realities dictate such a course of action.

A perfect example of this can be drawn from the natural language arena. If a researcher has attained success and notoriety through the use of detailed semantic primitives in natural language systems, then it is extremely likely that the researcher will attempt to develop products based on that approach. Assuming for the moment that all technical barriers are overcome, let us hypothesize the results of this technology-driven orientation.

The complexity of applying the resulting system to a new application will be very high because of the large number of complex definitions required. Furthermore, it is likely that only a limited number of people will be able to apply the system, due to the intricacy of the process. It follows that the resulting product cannot be sold as a generic utility, because the cost of application is so high. The company is left searching for specialized public-access applications that have sufficient volume to justify the cost of developing and implementing the system.

A better approach is one that first determines the constraints, such as cost, imposed by the marketplace and then finds an appropriate technology to live within those constraints. Unfortunately, the conviction with which most researchers hold their inventions causes them to take a technology-driven orientation, which ultimately constrains them to a small corner of the market.

Expert Systems Status

The current status of commercializing expert systems technology is very analagous to the early days of data processing. When computers were first being employed for commercial applications there were great expectations for their overall impact. But the complexities of the real world proved more difficult than expected. Eventually, after years of investment by companies that were convinced of the long-term strategic impact of computers, we saw successful data processing applications put into productive use.

Today the number of expert systems in actual productive use, as opposed to prototypes or systems in field-test, is still very small. Probably from 25 to 75 such systems existed as of January of 1985, far fewer than the impression given by recent accounts in the press. But once again, we have seen certain companies that are convinced of the strategic importance of AI investing in expert systems technology. This investment has taken the form of large consulting contracts with the AI startup companies as well as the creation of "Knowledge-Systems Engineering" departments that employ 50–100 internal "knowledge engineers," the programmers who build expert systems. Within the next two years there is no question that many of the hundreds of knowledge-based systems now in development or field testing will be put into productive use.

The applications are not likely to be the high-visibility, headline-making variety about which so much has been written. Rather, the bulk of these applications will be somewhat straightforward bread-and-butter applications that are related to the companies' lines of business. This is exactly what one might expect when expert systems are viewed as simply another kind of programming. As such, certain problems that

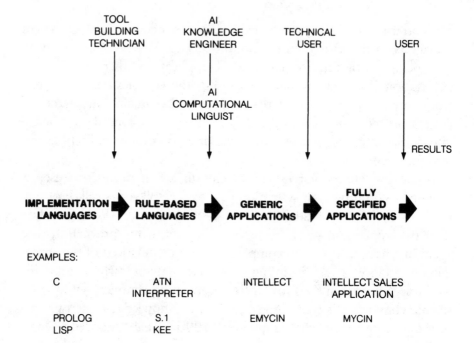

Figure 5.1   The Use of Different Types of Programming Languages in the Creation of Software Applications

were difficult to solve with third- or fourth-generation languages, are much easier to solve with the rule-based approach. What we will see are those companies gaining experience with expert systems and finding these easy "wins", based on this different approach to programming.

Choosing a Product Niche

Before looking at the strategies of different types of companies in the expert systems arena, it's helpful to examine more closely the various levels of possible AI products. Figure 5.1 shows the relationship between different programming languages and the roles they play in the overall software development process. Different languages not only serve different programming roles, but also serve different levels of users.

The "implementation languages," such as LISP, PROLOG, and C, are employed by technically proficient programmers to create the higher-level generic tools referred to as rule-based languages. These tools are the first examples of fifth-generation languages, and are generic in nature because they can be used to create applications across a wide variety of areas.

"Generic applications" are programs that function within particular problem areas such as natural language or machine configuration. They are generic in the sense that they can be applied to a number of different problems within their designated disciplines. For example, a natural language system could be employed to interface to a personnel database as well as to a marketing database. The creation of generic applications from rule-based languages requires the combined skills of the AI programmer, or "knowledge engineer, and the human expert in the application. doman.

The next stop in the process is the use of the generic application to build a fully specified application that can be used by nontechnical people to solve a particular problem. Examples of fully specified applications would include a natural language interface to a personnel database, or a computer configuration system for DEC minicomputers. The use of a generic application to create fully specified applications normally involves adding more definitions and facts to the knowledge base, a task that can conceivably be done by non-AI personnel. However, if the process also involves extensive modifications to the rules in the rule base, the chances that nonprogrammers can accomplish the task are considerably reduced.

This aspect can have grave implications on the commercial viability of the generic application product. For example, a natural language generic application that requires AI expertise to apply it to a new database will have a much more limited market than a product that could be applied by traditional programmers or even by the users themselves.

The final step in the product hierarchy is the use of the fully specified application by a nontechnical user to solve a problem. This might involve the asking of English questions to the natural language system to solve a personnel issue, or the consultation of an expert system to check the configuration of an order for a minicomputer system.

Note that the overall process shown in Figure 5.1 indicates how the tools developed in one area by technicians are used to create higher and higher-level tools, until a product accessible to the nontechnical user is developed. Vendors can sell tools at any level of this hierarchy. However, the market that is being addressed by each level is different because each demands a different level of technical expertise from its users.

There have been a relatively large number of start-up companies rushing to get into the expert systems marketplace at many of these various levels. The expert-system companies break down into three major categories: custom development firms, companies that sell knowledge-engineering tools, and vertical applications marketeers. In some instances there are companies that address more than one category.

Custom Development

The custom development market for expert systems is the most obvious means to exploit an understanding of the technology. Many of the former researchers in the field have become consultants to develop customized expert systems under contract for individual companies. In some cases, such as in the creation of Digital Equipment's *XCON* system, the work has involved outside consultants working with internal development teams to develop proprietary applications for use by the company.

The consulting approach is important for two reasons. First, it gets the researchers into the field, where they can learn about the realities of applying the rule-based technology. Second, it has the highest potential for developing commercially successful applications that can be put into production rather quickly. In this early stage of AI, it's still extremely important to establish some new successes that illustrate the payoff of the technology in actual commercial sites.

During the last three years, a considerable amount of custom development has been going on. While very few systems resulting from this development have yet been put in production, the success of the prototypes have been a major factor in many companies investing more heavily in AI technology. There are three major reasons why so few of the systems have been fielded.

The first is the inherent difficulty of the problems being addressed, as was discussed with regard to natural language products, but applies here as well. Classic AI problems have no clear specifications, nor do they have clear boundaries. It is hard to know when you have completed a sufficient portion of the solution to the degree necessary. The bad experiences many companies have had with traditional custom-programming contracts prompts them to be extremely cautious about signing up for products that can't even be clearly specified. Furthermore, there is a strong tendency among corporations to ask the consultants to address the firms' most difficult problems as a test of the technology. By contrast, in cases where the user company is involved in the development process there is a natural tendency to start with relatively easy problems.

The second reason for the long gestation period success of custom development is that the sale of these services is often made to a customer's research department. In the ideal company this is the proper place to bring in new technologies. Unfortunately, the same gap that exists between academic computer science and commercial data processing usually exists to a lesser degree between a company's research department and its production departments. This can make it surprisingly difficult to get a prototype application placed in production. Without the eventual support of the production departments, the application may never get into production.

The third reason for the long process involves the way the financial community looks upon companies that derive their revenue primarily from consulting services. There is no leverage from this type of activity because the company can only charge so much an hour for its services. Even though the hourly amount may be very high, the hour's work cannot be leveraged across more than one customer. If, on the other hand, the hour's work went into the development of a product that could be sold over and over again to several customers, then the work is more highly leveraged. All start-up companies are well advised that taking a product orientation rather than a consulting orientation will lead to greater interest from the financial community and therefore easier access to money at a better valuation.

From a corporate strategy viewpoint, this makes the product-orientation approach an extremely attractive one. But from the perspective of technological evolution, there is no doubt that the product orientation has slowed the success rate of applying the rule-based technology. The precious top technical resources of many start-up companies have been taken off custom applications and put on the development of lower-level generic products. In the long term this should benefit the technology, but the short-term effect is to delay the creation of successful applications.

Knowledge-Engineering Tools

In the rush to develop a product orientation, the products that could be most quickly developed were the knowledge-engineering toolkits. These tools, which essentially constitute the first of the fifth-generation programming languages, were simply the repackaging of the internal tools used within the company for custom development work. In some cases, considerable thought has been given to the nature of problems that users might experience with the tool and the support issues that would arise. In most cases, though, the toolkit products are simply higher-level languages that give novice users more than ample rope to hang themselves. There is a surprisingly large amount of competition in this market already. There is also a wide range in capability among the tools, but few distinguishing traits are visible on the surface. As such, the level of support provided by the vendor can be the critical factor in the successful purchase and use of any of the toolkits.

Another important aspect of the toolkits is that different tools have been designed to address different problems. This segmentation has come about as different research systems were converted into tools, but retained the orientation to the original problem they were designed to solve. One common grouping consists of *structured selection* (problems characterized by a finite set of solutions that can be solved by a rigid reasoning process); *planning* (problems such as project management); *design* (problems such as aircraft design); *constraint satisfaction* (problems such as the configuration of a computer system); and *model-based reasoning* (problems that require the use of diagrams or models for their solution).

The end effect of this segmentation is that toolkits designed to work with one type of problem may not work as well in solving problems outside their designated realms, and these limitations sometimes aren't very well publicized by the toolkit vendors. Try to get a toolkit designed for structured-selection problems to solve a constraint satisfaction problem, for instance, and you may not be able to do it. In fact, it may be impossible to achieve a solution in such a situation. This means that customers should not only evaluate the ease-of-use of toolkits and the amount of available support, but should also ensure that the products can be effectively applied to the problem at hand. Over the next several years we will undoubtedly learn much about what tools can be applied to which problems.

The market for toolkit products is already crowded and likely to get extremely price competitive in the near furture. This is because the toolkits are really the compilers or programming environments of fifth-generation programming languages. If the evolution of these languages is like that of the third-generation language compilers, then the market for the toolkits will belong to the hardware manufacturers, who have traditionally provided this level of software at very low rates along with their hardware.

If, on the other hand, the fifth-generation languages evolve in the way that the fourth-generation languages have, then prices may not fall. The vendors of fourth-generation products have been among the most successful independent software vendors. It has never been clear why the major hardware vendors haven't gotten very involved with selling fourth-generation products. Perhaps most didn't see them coming and it was too late to enter the market once they recognized its potential.

This is unlikely to be the case with fifth-generation languages. Several hardware manufacturers are already developing fifth-generation toolkits of their own, to be bundled in with their hardware in some cases. Digital Equipment, Texas Instruments, Hewlett-Packard, and others are active in this area. IBM has several research projects underway in this area, and has already announced toolkit products.

If these heavyweight vendors introduce products that are hard to distinguish from the other toolkits, it will further confuse the marketplace. With the expected lower prices from the hardware vendors, it is hard to imagine that many of the independent vendors will be able to effectively compete on product alone. One bright spot for the independents is that there will undoubtedly be room for vendors that provide a high level of support to their customers to increase the likelihood of success with the tools. Traditionally, the hardware manufacturers have been unable to provide this level of support.

Another difficulty implicit to the toolkit market is that today, most of the sales are to the research or planning departments of companies. As applications roll out into the field, different considerations, such as compatibility with existing applications, will come into play as the line organizations get involved. An important critical step that has yet to occur to any great degree is the sale of this type of product directly to the line organizations. These companies typically have their hands full already and, in general, are very slow to embrace new technologies.

One more revenue stream for the toolkit companies is that of professional education. To the degree that support becomes the critical component of success, these companies can exploit the need to train new programmers or retrain old programmers in the art of rule-based programming revolution. It's just one more way in which these companies can leverage their relatively scarce knowledge of the rule-based technology.

Vertical Applications

Another direction that the knowledge-engineering start-ups can take is the creation of vertical application products. These are programs written to solve a particular problem found within a single industry, such as insurance, or common to a single department across industries, such as personnel. The vertical application marketplace is very active for traditional software vendors, with the largest of the independent software companies, MSA, specializing in this area.

There have been fewer entrants into the vertical expert systems marketplace than one might expect, given the success that traditional software companies have had. This is because it is faster and easier to develop toolkit products than it is to develop real vertical applications. The toolkit product is not really an application of AI technology; it is simply the repackaging of the already existing programming tools.

To produce viable vertical applications requires truly solving a real-world problem using the rule-based technology. This means overcoming all the barriers already mentioned that are inherent to any AI problem; it also means doing this in such a way that the solution can be applied easily in a variety of corporate environments. Even for traditional programs, it is a lot easier to produce a solution for a specific problem in a specific environment than it is to provide a solution for a generic problem in a variety of environments. This is particularly true for the rule-based technology because so many of the company-specific aspects of the problem must be entered into the knowledge base by hand. This is similar in many ways to the problem encountered in developing a lexicon for a specific natural language application.

Another reason for the small number of vertical application expert system companies is the mindset of the academic-turned-entrepreneur. The commitment to build a vertical application is a commitment to fully understand the particular industry or generic problem being solved. The resulting company, if it is selling expert human resources software, resembles a human-resources consulting company much more than it resembles a leading-edge, high-technology venture. Most of these researchers, many of whom didn't completely break away from academia in the first place, simply can't envision themselves in this type of company. It is too far removed from the frontiers of the general technology.

All of this said, the potential financial rewards of building vertical expert systems is luring a number of qualified knowledge engineers into the commercial sector. We have already seen two vertical expert systems introduced in the past year from startup companies, APEX (Applied Expert Systems) and Palladian. It's too soon to tell how they will fare in the marketplace, but reviews from test sites sound promising. Over the next year or two we will see vertical applications of the expert system technology in the insurance and banking industries, as well as products for other financial applications. Since these products will be sold directly to the production departments that face the problems, rather than to the research or planning departments, there should be some very successful AI companies in this area.

The Role of Business

By serving as the most immediate users of AI, businesses play an especially important role in stimulating the rapid evolution of the technology. However, companies shouldn't expect to be employing AI extensively until they pass through what may be a fairly long lead time. A typical timeframe for most large organizations to effectively integrate new technologies into their operations is about five to ten years. For example, there are many organizations just now beginning to employ powerful, fourth-generation programming languages that have been available since the mid-1970s. The computer industry itself may be known for rapid change, but the process of establishing the widespread use of new technologies is surprisingly slow.

It's important to recognize the slow pace of this process, because it suggests that the time to begin to understand AI and experiment with the technology is now. Natural language processing, especially in conjunction with a voice-recognition capability, has the potential to radically transform the way information is used within a company. Expert systems will allow a host of strategically important problems to be solved that were not solvable with classical techniques. And, because of the long lead times required to incorporate these technologies, it will be hard for slow-starting companies to "catch up" to competitors who plunge into AI development and use early on.

Corporations investigating the use of AI technology are using various approaches. Some are forming strategic partnerships with AI companies. Others are beginning to experiment with AI in their own advanced technology divisions. Whatever the approach, it's important that the companies maintain a constant effort to move new applications from the research labs into their organizations as soon as field testing is completed. Exploiting rapid technological advances is one of the management challenges of the 1980s. Proper and timely incorporation of AI, in particular, will prove to be extremely critical in maintaining a competitive stance in virtually every business sector.

Societal Restrictions

We've devoted a fair amount of space to examining the commercial possibilities of artificial intelligence given the available technology. Doesn't this ignore the potential of society to place restrictions on the use of the technology? It does, but only because the field is still so new that it's difficult to imagine a near-term need for any restrictions beyond those imposed by the limitations of the technology itself. Even with these current limitations, AI can be a very powerful technology for effecting change. As such it's worth considering how people may impose some limits on the use of AI-based machines.

Probably the most visible example of machines impacting humans has been in the field of robotics. Even simple robots can replace people in some jobs, and AI *is* adding more intelligence and vision to the machines. As AI enhances the capabilities of robots, they will obviously become more utilitarian and a greater replacement threat to industrial workers. In one situation, General Motors is already training some of its displaced employees to perform maintenance on the robots that replaced them.

The phenomenon of technology displacing people has existed for some time, and AI has no exclusive claim in this process. Not just robotics, but office automation technologies, such as word processing, have changed and eliminated many jobs. That AI will possibly accelerate this trend is undeniable, but its gradual commercialization is unlikely to dramatically change the pace of technologically caused dislocation. At some future point AI *will* probably threaten a good number of jobs, and long-range planners would do well to factor its impact into their projections. In the final analysis, the perceived threat of AI isn't so much the numbers of jobs it will impact, but the type of jobs. AI is seen as a technology that may replace people whose jobs we view as prestigious, sensitive, and intellectually difficult—jobs for which no machine has ever before pretended to have proficiency.

Our hesitancy in accepting computers that can perform such high-level work is grounded largely in the question of trust. We know that no person is perfect, but it's certainly easier to accept a doctor's diagnosis as correct than to believe what a medical expert system might tell us. We have no track-record with which to evaluate such intelligent machines; until we do, we'll feel extremely uneasy about giving them great measures of authority or free reign. Fortunately, the evolution of artificial intelligence isn't likely to occur fast enough to raise the issue of an independently acting computer any time soon. In most situations, even relatively intelligent machines will serve as support tools for people, and will remain strictly within these people's jurisdiction.

Let's not forget, though, that we gladly accept the decisions of some lower-level machines. When watching the Los Angeles Olympics, wasn't it nice that the swimmers didn't fight about the results of their races, even though their times sometimes differed by mere 100ths of a second? Compare this with some of the human-judged events such as diving and gymnastics where human attributes as varied as concepts of beauty and political perspectives came into play. The split-second impartiality of an electronic timing system can seem very attractive by comparison. Not too many swimmers would exchange its accuracy for human timers holding stopwatches. Divers and gymnasts would probably appreciate a similar impartiality in the judging of their events, but there's no sign of any machines capable of delivering such a capability.

Just as some sporting events may never lend themselves well to judging by machines, many human tasks are extremely difficult to fully computerize, AI or not. In those that can be automated, our initial skepticism and uneasiness about the proliferation of machines is likely to fade as the computers gradually prove that they can be trusted, in some cases more than people.

But perhaps electronic timing systems are too benign an example of the incursion of machines in our lives. If they fail after all, no great harm will result. They are only measuring the time of a race, and should electronic glitches occur, a provision has been made for back-up human judges, as imperfect as they may be. Instead of sophisticated stopwatches, let's consider the automatic pilot systems installed in every commercial airplane. In most cases these systems can fly a plane as well or better than the human pilots, but we're not about to remove the human flight crews from our planes. Why not? Because we're not willing to trust the lives of thousands of people every day to the untended decisions of a machine, no matter how great its accuracy.

On the other hand, we're not about to pull out the automatic pilot equipment from every plane either. We recognize the value of these devices and understand that they can greatly aid the human pilots in navigation and flight control. The operative word here, of course, is "aid." Smart machines are fine as long as they know their place. And their place, we tend to believe, is always one of subservience to their human counterparts.

But is this relationship always so clear? If we leave planes behind and come down to the ground—underground, in fact—we're faced with a disturbing situation. Here we find subway systems, such as the Bay Area Rapid Transit network in San Francisco, that are heavily computerized. So heavily, in fact, that it's easy to conclude that the on-board human personnel play no more than a supporting role to the computers. If something goes wrong, fine, the BART employees are there to deal with the problem. Otherwise, sit back and let the computers schedule the trains, route them, collect the fares, and set the speeds.

Most BART riders seem satisfied with the resulting service, and not too many appear unwilling to trust the subway computers to convey them safely and efficiently from one location to another.

Will the balance of power in the air eventually shift to mirror that in the subways? Probably. But again, such a shift will be so gradual that most of us will be totally unaware that it is occurring. And, should human pilots one day be grounded because they have become unnecessary back-up systems for the computerized auto pilots, it will happen only in a world that long before accepted the reasonableness and inevitability of such a change. In other words, don't look for such a change to happen anytime soon.

Of course, the present-day systems we've been discussing have no AI component as yet. Perhaps it will be artificial techniques that some day in the distant future make automatic pilots powerful enough that they can actually replace people. Already, AI is starting to show up in applications that give people pause. Certainly a medical diagnosis system like *CADUCEUS* is enough to initiate questions about the permissable role of computers in health care. One area of AI development causes more concern than any other, however, and this concern is destined to grow along with the capabilities of AI. The field is military applications of artificial intelligence.

It should come as no surprise that the Defense Department has high hopes for the inclusion of AI in its support equipment and weapons systems. After all, the Defense Advanced Research Projects Agency, or DARPA, has been the prime benefactor of artificial intelligence research for most of the field's history. It was DARPA money that bankrolled the early forays into machine translation, and the support continued even after that seminal work met with failure. Much of the financing went to basic research projects that had no direct military applications, and it's only natural that the DoD is now attempting to realize some gain from its long-term investment. Some of the Defense Department's plans, however, raise people's worst fears about the potential misuse of AI.

These fears, like those we might experience if asked to ride in a plane flown only by an automatic pilot, relate to the degree of independence we're willing to give to intelligent machines. And if these machines are suddenly smart weapons that autonomously analyze battle situations and react accordingly, visions of Dr. Strangelove and doomsday machines begin to pop up in a lot of people's minds.

From the Defense Department's perspective, AI represents a crucial element for dealing in an expeditious manner with the complexities of modern warfare. Should we one day install in space the controversial "Star Wars" strategic weapons, they would require phenomenal computing power to identify and destroy incoming enemy missiles. Without AI programming techniques, the DoD argues, it's unlikely that such systems could ever achieve the necessary power to deal with such complex and time-critical situations.

Many are dismayed about this branch of AI research, however. A group calling itself Computer Professionals for Social Responsibility views with alarm the prospect granting autonomy to AI-based military systems. Three CPSR members writing on the dangers involved noted that all complex computer systems have limitations in reliability and pointed out that it's impossible to fully pretest the reliability of military systems meant to operate under the conditions of actual warfare. "The conclusion is inescapable," they wrote. "Autonomous weapons systems with great destructive power are dangerous because they increase the distance between human decision and decisive action. The greater the distance, the greater the likelihood of failure and the less predictable the consequences of failure" (*Boston Globe*, 7/30/84).

Not all of the DoD's plans for utilization of AI are as controversial as those in the area of autonomous weapons. But the use of AI in defense applications underscores a truism that is applicable to virtually all technologies, including artificial intelligence. That truism is that few technologies are inherently evil, but that any technology can be misused. That the potential for misuse is proportional to the power of the technology makes AI an area that warrants close scrutiny and supervision. But on balance, AI almost certainly offers more potential for good than for evil. Only time will tell whether this positive potential can be fully realized at the same time that the negative uses of AI are held in check. Determining which applications are positive and which are negative will require some tough, close calls, and these, in turn, will require a clear understanding of what AI can and cannot be expected to accomplish.

In the end, the application of artificial intelligence in our society can be seen as just one more landmark on the continuum of technology's progression. Like the technologies that preceded it, AI's acceptance will be won only grudgingly by the general public. That it doesn't differ in this sense from earlier advances can be seen from a story related by an elderly gentleman following his attendance at an AI seminar.

The man approached the speaker and explained how he had lived on a farm for most of his life. The family had an outhouse, and when the notion of moving a toilet into the house came along, it was a very upsetting concept. Once they had indoor plumbing for a while, though, the family realized it wasn't such a bad idea. Then came electricity, which, despite its obvious application around a farm, was not accepted gracefully. Television was rejected for a long time, but it finally settled in. "But the real kicker was the electric blanket," the gentleman said. "When they started replacing me in bed, keeping my wife warm, that was going too far."

Artificial intelligence is a lot like the electric blanket, in that it can replace people in some functions they would rather not relinquish. But, alarmists notwithstanding, the changes occasioned by AI will come slowly enough to give us plenty of time to adjust to them. The early changes will, for the most part, just make our lives easier, not less meaningful. Like the farmer probably discovered, it's nice to have some assistance when trying to stay warm on a cold winter's night.

6

Japan Inc.

- The Fifth Generation
- Parallel-Processing Goals
- Knowledge Bases
- The LISP Versus PROLOG Debate
- Revolutionary or Evolutionary?
- A History of Success
- Can Incompatibility Succeed?
- An Ace in the Hole

Even if artificial intelligence won't soon realize the more far-reaching and esoteric roles envisioned by some futurists for thinking machines, the field is promising enough to have lured many industrial countries into its waters. As with computer science in general, the United States leads its foreign competitors in AI research and development, but a number of countries have mounted substantial research programs with hopes of catching, and perhaps surpassing, the United States. Several European countries and the U.S.S.R. have such projects, but the United States looks most nervously over its shoulder to the Far East. There, Japan has mounted its so-called Fifth-Generation Project, a massive effort whose 1981 unveiling threw much of the world's AI community into turmoil.

What is it about Japan's plan that strikes such a vibrant chord? Government funding over the 10-year span of the Fifth-Generation Project is expected to range from $200 to $500 million, and participating Japanese companies may double that amount. But this backing isn't so great that it makes other AI bankrolls pale by comparison. The Moscow Academy of Sciences allocated an initial $100 million to its current five-year plan for computing, which has a heavy emphasis on AI topics. The European Economic Community is coordinating a 10-year, $2.6 billion computer and AI program called ESPRIT (European Strategic Program for Research and Development in Information Technology). And some of the individual EEC members have their own domestic projects. One, Britain's Alvey program, will provide $300 million over five years to sponsor up to 50 percent of the cost of collaborative research between university and industry scientists.

What Japan has that the other AI competitors don't is a clear mission, well-defined product goals, and an impressive history of success in other computer fields. While most AI programs, including those in the United States, are more or less shotgun approaches to the field, the Japanese have narrowed their sights on specific targets. They have also chosen a limited number of tools and methods to attain their goals, rather than experiment with a variety of approaches. By so doing, they hope to dispense with the meandering advances common in other countries and travel on an express route to the next generation of computer hardware and software. Interestingly, this approach essentially places all the bets for success on one number, an unusual strategy for a people often said to prefer risk aversion to gambling on uncertainties. The success of the Japanese in attaining their goals by following their chosen path is by no means certain.

Upon scrutiny, in fact, certain aspects of the Japanese approach seem misguided and unnecessarily constricting. To understand these shortcomings, we must first examine Japan's strategy for leap-frogging the rest of the world in the ongoing computer race. The next chapter, which examines the status and the direction of U.S. artificial intelligence work, will further help in establishing that, while the Japanese AI work is important, and while it will almost certainly conquer some computer frontiers, it is doubtful that Japan will manage to completely outdistance its competitors in this field.

The Fifth Generation

Shortly after it announced its Fifth-Generation Project, Japan began assembling a group of about 40 young computer scientists to achieve the plan's lofty goals. This group was culled from several of Japan's major computer companies and laboratories by Kazuhiro Fuchi, who continues to lead the project as director of the Institute for New Generation Computer Technology (ICOT). Other institutions involved with the effort are the University of Tokyo, Nippon Telephone and Telegraph's Musashino Laboratories, and the Ministry of International Trade and Industry's (MITI's) Electrotechnical Laboratory, which Fuchi formerly directed. Eight firms form a consortium backing and participating in the project; they are Fujitsu Ltd., NEC Corp., Hitachi Ltd., Mitsubishi Electronic Corp., Toshiba Corp., OKI Electric Industry Co. Ltd., Matsushita Electric Industry Co. Ltd., and Sharp Corp. In other words, the Japanese are again banking on their triad of government, industry, and university cooperation that has served them so well in other development efforts.

While the fifth-generation team—which now consists of about 70 researchers—constitutes an impressive array of talent and financing power, the project's goals are nothing short of staggering. The project is broken into three development stages, with two intermediate plateaus scheduled en route to the 1991 summit. Unlike much of the current AI work, which tends to reside primarily in the software realm, Japan's goals encompass both hardware and software advances. In essence, Japan is arguing that software alone won't be enough to fully realize AI's potential. They therefore plan to break away from the existing forms of computers, and to develop new machine architectures that will best support their fifth-generation software.

Central to Japan's hardware plans is the concept of an "inference engine." As we saw in earlier chapters, much of AI is based on rules of logic that serve to step through known facts to arrive at nonprogrammed conclusions. So far, these inferencing techniques have been embodied in software simply because traditional computer hardware is designed to perform much lower-level operations.

All of today's computers achieve their power through simple arithmetic computations that are performed at very high speeds. Because some basic math operations are common to most tasks a computer performs, electronic components have been specifically built to perform certain arithmetic operations. Such "hardwired" functions operate much more quickly than like functions programmed in software, because they can be initiated by a single command and performed at electronic speed. Conversely, software-based functions require several commands to execute and tie up the computer's main processor, which must deal with the software functions itself rather than relying upon another hardware device to automatically perform the operations.

The inherent speed limitations of functions programmed in software have long been recognized, and the trend in computer development has been to place as many functions in hardware as possible. For example, fundamental data communications and graphics processing operations are being placed on computer chips that can be plugged into computers for faster processing of these applications.

Not all functions can be set in hardware because such hardwiring makes for inflexibility and can cause obsolescence as methods and operations evolve. Thus, even though the Japanese plan to develop inferencing hardware, this hardware will perform only low-level, commonly needed functions. The creation of the rule base and the basic facts will remain software based. But by building equipment that automatically searches for rules with relevant consequents and then invokes a search to prove their antecedent condition, the Japanese expect to create machines that operate on large knowledge bases at incredible rates.

To measure the speed of these future computers, the Japanese have coined the term "logical inferences per second" or "LIPS." Traditional arithmetic computers are rated by the number of "instructions per second" that they process. It requires many machine instructions to achieve a single logical inference; as a rough measure, a 10-MIPS (million instructions per second) traditional processor can perform about 1000 LIPS. The fastest of today's supercomputers can perform several hundred MIPS, and even personal computers have begun to approach the 1-MIP level. Japan's inference machines, on the other hand, are slated to achieve a mind-boggling one billion *LIPS* by 1991!

Parallel-Processing Goals

How can Japan hope to create a new type of machine that will so exceed the power of today's fastest computers? Key to this plan is the successful development of parallel processing—the use of multiple processors within a single machine to "gang up" on each problem. The notion of parallel processing isn't specific to the Japanese; theoreticians and computer scientists have been working on such computers for years. The Japanese are the first, however, to propose building such machines for the specific purpose of performing inferencing operations.

All but a few computers manufactured today are single-processor machines that process information sequentially. Some operate at incredible speeds, but they face a finite boundary: at some point, the capability of a single processor to move electronic signals among its components approaches physical limits. Some supercomputers such as those from Cray and Control Data are nearing this upper boundary, and these companies and others have already taken initial steps into the realm of parallel processing.

These steps have only been tentative, however, because it's extremely difficult to simultaneously apply several processors to a single task. Although many factors contribute to this difficulty, two fundamental problems involve how to efficiently divide a task among multiple processors and how to control the flow of information through such a multiprocessor machine. For example, if two of the processors need the same piece of data to compute a result, one must wait for the other to use the data and free it before proceeding with its computation. Often the information required to solve part of a problem must first be computed by the machine. How can designers ensure that such information is produced by one processor in a parallel machine in time to feed it to a sister processor that requires the result?

Several schemes have been devised to solve such parallel-processing problems. For instance, copies of required data can be made available to several processors at once. As for the control of information passing through a multiple-processor machine, one technique favored by the Japanese is that of "dataflow." Developed by Jack Dennis, an MIT computer scientist, dataflow works like a series of parallel water pipes that connect at certain nodes. A single node may have several pipes leading into it and several exiting, but the node can't pass any water along until it has first been filled with water from each of its entering pipes. Once this water has been provided, the node performs its function and passes water along its output pipes to the next node or series of nodes.

In a dataflow architecture, the pipes carry instructions and pieces of data and the nodes are processors that perform specific operations using the instructions and data. In a well-designed system, the processing nodes are arranged so that the data needed by each node is provided by one or more nodes preceding it. The node waits until all the pipes entering it have provided the necessary information. It then performs its designated operation and passes the result of the operation out to the lower nodes that require the data. This process imposes an orderly flow of information between the processing nodes, ensuring that none can perform its function until those that should logically precede it have performed theirs.

Although dataflow and some competing schemes for handling parallel processing appear relatively straightforward, their implementation has proven difficult. Those trying to implement them so far have been dealing with the known world of data calculations, not the unknown territory of symbolic inferencing.

Recognizing the barriers they must overcome to meet their hardware goals, the Japanese are moving a step at a time. They have designed and built a single-processor, sequential inference machine called the PSI. Mitsubishi is manufacturing this computer and began marketing it in Japan in late 1985. Now that this intermediate objective has been met, ICOT and its member companies are making an all-out effort to produce a parallel-processing version of the device.

In this effort, the Japanese expect to be able to capitalize on the fact that many AI tasks, such as expert-system processing, are inherently parallel; all the rules that might apply to a given problem can be applied in parallel, for instance. This eliminates many of the efficiency considerations mentioned earlier. This fact makes the ICOT researchers hopeful that, far from being more difficult to apply unproven parallel processing to unproven knowledge engineering tasks, their job will be simplified by the natural parallelism of the applications. It's in the traditional world of numeric processing, which by nature is often sequential, that the application of parallel processing proves most difficult, they believe.

Knowledge Bases

A key ingredient of such fifth-generation machines is the ability to store vast amounts of knowledge. Such knowledge bases differ from traditional computer databases in that the former consist of both an unstructured set of facts and inference rules for determining new facts. Both knowledge bases and databases can be measured by the number of bytes they hold. Current databases range from a few thousand bytes on personal computers to hundreds of millions of bytes on corporate mainframe systems. Not ones for shirking the difficult, the Japanese predict that fifth-generation machines might store anywhere from 10 billion to 100 billion bytes of knowledge. ICOT has already designed a relational database management machine called Delta that consists of four linked dual-processor elements and stores 20 billion bytes of facts.

Of course, full-blown knowledge bases will contain not just facts, but rules—as many as 20,000 rules for particular expert systems. They would also hold extensive vocabularies (perhaps 10,000 words) for use in natural language processing.

Because the Japanese are also placing heavy emphasis on speech recognition, the knowledge base would also store voice patterns of words for comparison with the patterns generated by an operator's vocal commands or entries. And since image processing is expected to be a crucial capability for future AI systems, the fifth-generation knowledge base will be called upon to hold the patterns of any pictures or scenes that its TV-camera eye might be asked to identify. In this regard, the quip that a picture is worth 1000 words has an ironic twist: the storage requirement for placing an image into a computer's memory dwarf the space needed to hold 1000 words.

The LISP Versus PROLOG Debate

All these storage requirements will make for an incredibly large and complex knowledge base. To build parts of it and to interface to the hardware inference engine, the Japanese have chosen to work initially with a European-developed computer language called PROLOG. PROLOG has its roots in predicate logic, and is viewed by ICOT director Fuchi as a more advanced language than LISP, the 25-year-old language still employed by most American AI researchers. Both are simply low-level implementation languages with which fifth-generation languages and systems can be built. As such, the choice of one over the other is not as critical as, say, the choice of one fifth-generation toolkit over another. Still, it's worth looking at Japan's choice of PROLOG as a foundation upon which is being built more advanced logic programming languages and dedicated hardware.

Japan's embrace of PROLOG represented a fairly bold step at the time. Prior to the Fifth Generation's inception, PROLOG had only a small following in Europe. The world leaders in AI, the Americans, had worked almost exclusively with the older LISP language in attaining their leadership position.

PROLOG is a somewhat higher-level language than LISP, and as such it has some advantages upon which the Japanese believe they can capitalize. One of PROLOG's basic strengths is the simplicity of its nomenclature. PROLOG statements are more easily understandable than LISP, and, being a logic-programming language, the PRO-LOG language itself makes logical connections between related facts. In this regard, PROLOG is different from LISP, which is a "functional programming language," and uses a different type of notation. LISP essentially applies various mathematical functions to different symbols, which can be anything, not just numbers.

J. Alan Robinson, the research director at Syracuse University's Center for Advanced Technology, has been quoted as saying that the difference between LISP and PROLOG is that "functional programming is deduction with equations" while logic programming is "computing with conditional sentences" (*Science News*, 6/2/84). Despite their differences, however, both languages share the ability to state relationships between different "objects" and can both infer follow-on relationships.

Despite its relative ease of use, PROLOG does have some problems. Because of its inherent ties to strict mathematical logic, PROLOG might have some difficulty in exercising the less-precise, or "fuzzy," logic that AI problem-solving often requires. One PROLOG feature that serves it well in some circumstances—a built-in search mechanism that navigates through the complex trees of a program's if/then rules—sometimes works against the language. Because the language itself automatically initiates and performs these searches, it's difficult for the programmer or the system operator to control the search and redirect or limit it. The time required for indiscriminate searches can grow exponentially as the knowledge base grows and the number of facts and relationships increases. For knowledge bases of the size contemplated by the Japanese for their fifth-generation computers, the implications of uncontrollable PROLOG searches can be disastrous.

Of course, the ICOT researchers are as aware of PROLOG's limitations as they are of its strengths. Director Fuchi has been quoted as saying, "If we want a logic-programming language there is little to choose from but PROLOG" (*Science News*, 6/2/84). As such, ICOT has used PROLOG merely as a springboard to jump into the development of more sophisticated logic-programming languages. The laboratory has already produced the first level of its KL (kernal language) language, designated KL0. This runs on the personal sequential inference machines designed by ICOT and provides several extensions that address many of PROLOG's shortcomings. ICOT has also developed an even higher-level logic-programming language called ESP, and has used it to construct an advanced operating system called SIMPOS for the PSI computers.

Likewise, other nations' computer scientists are producing their own improved versions of PROLOG or totally different logic programming languages. One effort by Robinson at Syracuse involves a language he calls "Super-LOGLISP," in which he is attempting to combine the best features of functional and logic programming.

In any case, what has received much billing as a crucial distinction between the Japanese and the American AI work—the use of PROLOG or LISP—is in many ways a red herring. Robinson is correct in recognizing that each language has its advantages. The only way to approach any particular AI problem is to evaluate its demands and then choose the best programming tool available for meeting those demands. If the Japanese were totally wedded to the current implementation of PROLOG, or if the Americans refused to consider anything beyond LISP, it's possible the choice of language might make a small difference in the AI race. But neither situation is the case, and it seems highly unlikely that the success or failure of one country's AI program will turn on the program's preference for one language over another.

Revolutionary or Evolutionary?

Even though ICOT's attraction to logic-based programming is unlikely to sway the AI balance one way or another, their method of choosing PROLOG as a foundation language says something important about the Japanese strategy. Basically, it highlights the decision to pick a narrowly defined set of tools and a specific set of product goals. The issue, as with PROLOG, isn't one of picking the right or wrong tool or goal. It's simply that by following a focused approach, the Japanese are limiting their options. (It must be noted that ICOT doesn't represent the total spectrum of AI research and development ongoing in Japan. Japanese companies and universities, both ICOT-associated and not, are pursuing their own AI projects, some of which break from the direction set by ICOT. Still, the Fifth-Generation Project represents the "official" Japanese strategy, and ICOT's initiatives carry a lot of weight in influencing the country's corporate research goals and the universities' computer course content.) Japan has a relatively brief history of AI work compared to the Americans and the Europeans, so how can ICOT have confidence in the suitability of its choices? Have the rest of us been so blind that we've failed to see the true path to widespread AI realization?

The answers to these questions rest on the understanding that Japan has chosen to pursue a revolutionary approach to AI, whereas most other countries continue to follow an evolutionary one. In some ways, this difference is inevitable. The Americans and the Europeans, after all, have been researching AI subjects for close to 30 years. While brief by some standards, 30 years bridges almost the full-span of modern computer history. It has certainly been long enough for many AI branches and techniques to evolve. Each has its adherents, and little other than LISP has achieved a widespread status as a "right" tool or method. The point is that PROLOG is just like any one of 50 other ideas that people have had that are interesting and hold some promise: not one of these ideas appears good enough to totally ignore the other 50.

If the United States, and even Europe, have any major advantage over Japan in the development of AI it's their tendency to examine the full breadth of available ideas. It seems unlikely that many of the AI researchers in these countries would sacrifice their broad, hands-on AI experience for the questionable advantage of partaking in a narrow, well-directed quest to win some arbitrarily defined fifth-generation race. As for the so-called race, it was on long before Japan entered the picture. While the Japanese project has set some impressive and highly visible goals, it hardly encompasses all of the research paths long travelled in AI.

All that said, the Japanese project shouldn't be written off as insignificant. It *is* an ambitious and revolutionary plan that will almost certainly achieve some success. If, by some chance, Japan has chosen exactly the right tools and the right goals, perhaps it could actually pull off the AI coup that so many fear. ICOT itself has always discounted such a scenario, and claims to be merely researching AI and advanced computer technology in order to improve the lot of people everywhere.

The odds against an overwhelming success seem almost insurmountable. For one thing, Japan's stated goals are so high that even the ICOT researchers have many doubts about their ability to attain them within their 10-year timeframe. While the goals encompass many fundamental and generic products that could serve in numerous AI applications, they by no means encompass the whole AI spectrum.

When all is said and done, Japan was forced into its revolutionary approach just as the United States and Europe are obliged to stay largely within their evolutionary model. Japan correctly recognized the potential that artificial intelligence holds, and the country saw the field as a means to finally take the computing initiative away from the United States. But the Japanese had no time to spare in realizing this objective, since AI work in other countries was already well established. Thus the narrow-focus Fifth-Generation Project, which will no doubt achieve some success, will also suffer from its inability to encompass the entire AI picture.

The distinction between the Japanese approach and those of other countries has an interesting analog in AI itself. Much like the parallel-processing inferencing engines the Japanese are building, the Americans and the Europeans are travelling in parallel along hundreds of paths to achieve multiple goals. This can be a lengthy process. If the way to speed it involves eliminating or ignoring much of the knowledge in the knowledge base, it may be best to continue the broad, unstructured search. The Japanese, on the other hand, have constructed a narrow knowledge base and have asked it a limited number of questions. If the knowledge they utilize has been deftly chosen, it may form a direct path to the rapid solution of their questions. If gaps exist in the knowledge base, the search may run into a dead end rather than succeeding. If so, they will have to back up and start again.

A History of Success

Can we feel comfortable in the knowledge that Japan is new to the AI game and has been forced to make hard choices to make itself a contender? At one point, Japan was relatively new to consumer electronics, to automobile manufacturing, and to steel production. Clearly that didn't stop the country from quickly overtaking and surpassing its established competitors in these areas. However, artificial intelligence is a special case in several ways.

The most obvious difference between the AI race and those that the Japanese have already run and won, is that this time Japan's competitors know the race exists. By publicizing its Fifth-Generation Project, the Japanese served a notice to the world that even the most complacent couldn't ignore. After repeated losses to Japan in other economic areas, complacency had become something of a rare commodity anyway. When Japan announced its intentions to effectively obsolete much of the existing computer industry, it naturally generated a protective response. The United States and every other country involved with computers and AI have taken the Japanese challenge seriously, and that reaction alone has altered the scenario of earlier Japanese conquests.

Even more important to an analysis of Japan's potential for success is the understanding that AI remains largely a research-level discipline. While much progress has been made, AI is not a finished product that can be simply packaged and marketed in a variety of ways. As the Japanese project itself makes clear, much innovation and development is still required before we can begin to view AI as something able to seriously threaten the existing base of computer hardware and software. It's in this regard that the Japanese find themselves in unexplored territory for the first time.

While it's easy to over-generalize, it's apparent that Japan's demon-strated strengths in world economic competition have been largely in the areas of engineering and manufacturing. The Japanese have also excelled in identifying new markets and in applying existing technology to exploit these untapped areas. They may not have invented the transistor, but they were certainly the first to fully take advantage of its potential. Their dominance of the consumer electronics field resulted. Although the assembly line and robotics are American innovations, Japan was the first to effectively combine the two across a wide range of manufacturing operations. The resulting cost efficiencies and prod-uct quality—and the effect on competing products—are well known in the automobile and electronics worlds.

Still, some argue, the Japanese have never shown much of an ability to innovate, to truly create and develop totally new technologies. That flaw, say the skeptics, at least throws the Fifth-Generation Project's chances for success into serious question. After all, we're not talking here about "reverse engineering," where people work backwards from a finished product to learn about and mimic the product's technology. Success in AI requires breaking ground that none have so far touched, say the critics, and the Japanese have demonstrated no capability for such innovation.

The flaws exist more in the skeptics' arguments than in Japan's capabilities. The line between innovation in manufacturing and in technology development isn't always a clear one, and the Japanese are undisputed masters of the former. Recognizing that they have something to prove to the world, the Japanese are marshalling a new type of talent to pursue the fifth-generation goals. In a tacit admission that the young tend to be more innovative than the old, the ICOT scientists and engineers have been selected as much for their youth as for their skills. The average age of the ICOT staff is about 30. Placing so important a project on the shoulders of such young researchers represents a sharp break with the traditional Japanese approach of gradually integrating its young into the rigid, homogenous structure of Japan's old-line companies.

This approach doesn't guarantee success, of course. In fact, too much reliance on the young could prove troublesome as the project nears the product stage. Building prototype products is one thing, determining how to apply the products in the marketplace is another. While Japan has so far excelled in such technology application, it's not clear if the Fifth-Generation Project is making enough use of its seasoned industry expertise in this area. People can talk all they want about the advantages of Japan's government, industry, and university cooperation, but if too much reliance is placed on young researchers right out of college, some of that advantage might be lost. The danger of such an oversight is undoubted something the Japanese recognize. Of more importance is their willingness to utilize methods that are revolutionary to their society in order to achieve their revolutionary goals.

Even if the Japanese gamble succeeds and they demonstrate to themselves and their competitors that innovation isn't limited to the Western world, innovation and development take time. Having an existing technology and turning it around quickly into a product is one thing, developing the technology is another. The ICOT researchers have given themselves 10 years to attain their goals, but that probably won't be enough time to fully realize them. In the meantime, the rest of the world is not sitting still.

Can Incompatibility Succeed?

Lost in much of the analysis of the Fifth-Generation Project is one of its most basic, and risky, tenets. By choosing to develop totally new hardware to accelerate their AI software, the Japanese plan to make a major break with the existing computer world. That world is dominated by IBM Corp., and every country, including Japan, has long worked within a computing environment largely dictated by the giant U.S. company. While many disagree with some of the strictures this situation imposes, it has some undeniable advantages. Most fundamental of these is the creation of a compatibility standard of sorts. Each computer manufacturer goes its own way in certain areas, but they can always fall back on the IBM standard if they want to exchange information or interface in other ways to the majority of the world's computers.

In part, this compatibility goes beyond IBM. At its most basic level, it lies on a foundation of data stored in binary form and manipulated by sequential, numeric processors. To fully succeed in their AI effort, Japan must obsolete much of that approach, turning its back on the vast installed base of computers and databases. With the Japanese approach, future customers will be required to invest in new hardware as well as software. There are pluses and minuses to that approach, but mostly minuses.

In a way, the Japanese are saying, "Not only are we going to solve the most important problems facing AI, but with our hardware we're going to solve them in such a way that nobody else can do it on traditional hardware." Or, "We're going to solve the problems so much better than anyone else can, that customers will be forced to buy our hardware." That's an incredibly risky strategy. If it succeeds, Japan gains a lock on the hardware marketplace. If it fails, Japan might end up with some very expensive solutions that others can come close to achieving in more cost-effective ways.

If the potential customers for AI products are in areas where they don't have any need to interface to existing computers or their databases, the Japanese chances for success improve. In such standalone applications, why not buy the best hardware and software available? But most computer applications will need to have links to other computers and data, and achieving such links with revolutionary products may prove difficult. Bridges between different types of computers can be built over communications networks, but the greater the differences between two machines, the more imposing the bridge building becomes. So, if someone can perform 90 percent of an AI job by putting a software solution on a classical computer, that route may prove the most acceptable to the marketplace. If the solutions to a large number of problems require new hardware architectures, the Japanese might have some advantage, but not a total one.

For while the Japanese have made an explicit link between parallel-processing hardware and AI applications, they are not alone in the effort to develop parallel machines. Hundreds of parallel-processing research efforts exist around the world, although not all are focused entirely on the AI realm. The United States and Britain have several prototype parallel computers already, and several U.S. companies already sell machines containing multiple processors. American and European AI researchers who desire to explore the use of parallel processing therefore have the option to do so.

The distinction is one between an evolutionary, multihued approach and a revolutionary, narrowly focused one. Incompatibility is a big issue, not something to snub. Paradoxically, the Japanese may have to devote as much time and attention to retrofitting to the existing world as they do to their attempts to break away from it.

An Ace in the Hole

Let's assume the worst scenario that might befall Japan—an extremely unlikely scenario at best. Say their grand plans are all for naught, they fail to meet their intermediate and their final Fifth-Generation goals, and they demonstrate a notable inability to develop any new technology. Meanwhile, the rest of the world in general, and the United States in particular, gradually progress in their melange of AI projects. One software application is developed here, another there, and the move toward parallelism continues apace. Will Japan suddenly be out of the picture?

Hardly. In fact, such a bleak scenario for the Japanese places them in the same situation they've exploited in other areas with incredible success. Even if they fail to lead the world in AI research and development, what's to keep the Japanese from picking up the fruits of other countries' labor and applying it most effectively in the market? Nothing. And it's in this regard that the Japanese threat in AI is most real.

It could be easy for the rest of the world to become so caught up with beating Japan to the Japanese-defined Fifth-Generation goals that it neglects the need to bring current AI technology to market in useful and creative ways. Much AI technology *does* already exist. It makes no sense to ignore what's already available to us and turn all our attention to pursuing some future goals. If the past is any lesson, the Japanese are unlikely to make such a mistake. At their heart, the problems faced by AI aren't pure research problems, but are problems associated with *applying* the technology.

Given Japan's history, how are they likely to exploit AI? First, in manufacturing, where they already lead most of the world. Artificial intelligence has obvious relevance to robotics and to the building of factory knowledge bases, and Japan will probably move quickly to take advantage of AI's potential in such areas. The result: once again, Japan stands to jump ahead of its competition in all types of manufacturing. In this sense, a little AI knowledge can go a long way.

Likewise, the Japanese may bring to bear their skills of identifying new markets where even rudimentary AI can be usefully applied. If they can successfully produce AI-based products that meet needs unidentified by other countries, the question of who first developed the technology can quickly become a moot point.

It's therefore imperative that AI research and development efforts not lose sight of the application of their work. Part of the AI community must continually strive to conquer higher summits; without such a search for new insights and techniques the field would stagnate. Another part of the community must be aware of the commercial world and of that world's needs. Without the latter awareness, the Americans and the Europeans might find that, once again, they've won the technological battle, but lost the economic war.

7

Maintaining the U.S. Edge

- The Government's Role
- A Consortium of Competitors
- Handicapping MCC's Prospects
- The Entrepreneurial Lure
- A Risky Business
- Educational Shortcomings

With its Fifth-Generation Project, Japan has clearly set some ambitious goals. While it seems unlikely that all these will be realized within the project's 10-year framework, few in the U.S. AI community advocate ignoring the Japanese initiative. In fact, if anything, the U.S. response to the Fifth Generation has been one of overreaction. While scrambling to meet the perceived Japanese challenge, it's easy to forget that the Fifth-Generation Project itself represents a response by Japan to counter the already substantial U.S. activity in the AI field.

Since there was already a strong base of AI research in the United States, it's difficult to disentangle which of this country's current activities are direct responses to Japan's project, and which are merely continuations of existing AI trends. But there has been a response, even if it's difficult to quantify. The history of Japan's success in consumer electronics, automobiles, and steel certainly makes prudent the U.S. perception that the Fifth Generation could be a serious threat to our dominance in the overall computer field. With the information processing market accounting for approximately three percent of the U.S. gross national product, or about $88 billion per year, the threat is nothing to take lightly.

Probably the most visible aspect of Japan's approach to world markets such as AI is its reliance on close cooperation between the governmental, industrial, and educational sectors. This triumvirate is seen as something that gives Japan an unfair advantage over the segmented U.S. model. But in the computer field, the individual U.S. sectors of government, industry, and universities have already achieved impressive accomplishments in their own rights. An examination of the U.S. scene indicates a growing willingness to permit, and even encourage, closer cooperation between these three sectors.

The U.S. government, which has long funded industry and university AI research through the Defense Advanced Research Projects Agency (DARPA), is beefing up that funding partially in response to the Fifth-Generation Project. The government is also relaxing its antitrust watchdog role and permitting more cooperation between competing companies. Meanwhile, corporations and universities are jointly attempting to ensure that college curricula are more in line than they have been in the past with industrial trends and requirements.

In combination with these changes, the United States has its standby strengths of powerful corporations such as IBM and, on the other end of the spectrum, its unique entrepreneurial environment. The large and small U.S. companies have yet to demonstrate they can dominate the AI field in the same manner in which they have dominated much of the world's existing computer industry. There's no guarantee that the untested ICOT program will prove more successful, and should the Japanese paradigm prove the best for dealing with AI research and development, the United States is forming similar models with which to compete.

The Government's Role

Those concerned about the Japanese government's support for AI research and development should not forget that the relatively advanced state of U.S. AI is almost wholly a result of 20 years of DARPA funding. That funding is steadily increasing. DARPA's current program, the Strategic Computing Initiative (SCI), is tentatively budgeted for $600 million over its first five years. The SCI received $50 million during the 1984 fiscal year, its first year of funding, $95 million for FY85, and $150 million in FY86. This compares favorably to the Fifth-Generation Project's funding, which may never attain the projected financing goal of $850 million over its 10-year lifetime.

The importance of DARPA's AI funding was noted in an analysis performed by the Congressional Office of Technology Assessment. In 1982, the study said, approximately 90 percent of the funding for artificial intelligence and parallel processing research came from the Pentagon. This percentage will likely drop as venture capitalists become more involved in bankrolling AI start-ups and as major corporations pump more of their own money into AI research, but the total level of government support will almost certainly continue to grow.

The Strategic Computing Initiative shares some attributes beside funding levels with the Fifth-Generation Project. Like the Japanese effort, the DARPA plan is extremely ambitious, and has been criticized as such. Some AI researchers believe that the SCI depends too much on "scheduled breakthroughs" to meet its objectives. Others look at the range of research encompassed by the plan, which includes goals in microelectronics, computer architectures, and software as well as AI, and question the ability of even DARPA to coordinate and direct the project. Still others wonder whether, even with the perfect execution of the plan, AI is capable of accomplishing some of the tasks DARPA has set for it.

Some important distinctions also exist between DARPA's role as a backer of AI and the role played by Japan's Ministry of International Trade and Industry. The most obvious difference is evident from the names of the funding agencies. MITI's goal is to finance and coordinate the development of commercial products that might shift the market's balance of power. DARPA is increasingly concerned with AI's role in weapons that may shift the military balance of power.

This was not always the case. In the early years of AI, DARPA was further removed from the actual application of the technologies whose research it funded. Within the guidelines of the SCI, however, the emphasis has shifted more toward applied research; the project's main objectives involve the development of AI-based military system proto-types that will demonstrate the feasibility of the underlying technolo-gies to the various armed service branches. The planned systems include an unmanned automated vehicle for the Army, an Air Force "pilot's associate" that would help fly fighter jets in combat situations, and a battle management system for the Navy that would monitor and manage aircraft flight patterns and the movements of associated support ships.

Much of the funding for work associated with these projects is still directed to the development of generic technologies, and in that sense, the fruits of the research are likely to have some commercial market applications. Some argue that MITI, which can devote all of its funding toward commercial applications, sits in a more powerful position than DARPA in influencing the market's dynamics. Because of this difference in focus many in the U.S. AI community gain little comfort from a simple comparison of Japanese and U.S. government funding levels.

Since both the SCI and the Fifth-Generation Project combine artificial intelligence and parallel processing research, it raises an obvious question: How important is the realization of parallel processing to the achievement of useful AI implementations? If the importance is major, can we expect to see powerful AI systems prior to the general availability of parallel machines? These are complex issues, but the role of parallel computing as a key prerequisite for powerful AI doesn't stand up well under scrutiny.

This fact is best illustrated by the computer chess example. There are two schools of thought about how to best create a winning computer-chess system. One is to increase the processing speed, permitting the computer to win through the brute force examination of hundreds of thousands of possible moves and countermoves. The other approach is to increase the computer's skill by giving it sophisticated strategic knowledge.

In fairness, both approaches have shown some success. High speed can buy you something, but in chess the exponential growth of possible moves eventually overwhelms even the fastest of computers. Since human chess masters—who can't consider anywhere near the number of moves a computer can—are still able to use skill to beat the best computer-chess systems it shows that speed has its limitations in AI. Admittedly, few, if any, present-day AI applications have anywhere near the exponential growth of options inherent in chess. The builders of chess-playing programs also have a major advantage over the developers of natural language and expert systems. This advantage is one that gives chess the ability to be solved, in part, through brute speed. Namely, chess has a limited set of legal moves, and these are well understood.

With a normal knowledge-based system you can't usually tell it, "Here are all the legal possibilities. Now blindly search through them." The legal moves of medical diagnosis are not as well understood as the legal moves of chess. A major part of the developer's job, therefore, is to choose the applicable rules and to make sure the set is complete enough to solve the problems the system will face. If this AI portion of the system isn't well conceived, no amount of brute force processing will solve the problem.

The level of detail required in building an adequate rule base for an AI system can be staggering. Consider, for example, a single rule from the *XCON* computer-configuration system:

IF   the most current active context is assigning a power supply,
       and a UNIBUS adaptor has been put in a cabinet,
       and the position it occupies in the cabinet (its nexus) is known,
       and there is a space available in the cabinet for a power supply for
       that nexus,
       and there is an available power supply,
       and there is no H7101 regulator available,
THEN   add an H7101 regulator to the order.

This rule illustrates the level of detail required in defining a commercial-grade rule base. Every possible configuration issue must be resolved by a rule such as this. As is apparent from the *XCON* rule, covering all the possibilities is the real challenge. Another set of rules must apply for all the conditions under which this rule might fail. Being certain that some situations haven't been left out is an exhaustive process. Such holes are usually not discovered until the system encounters that particular situation, often while running in production. The issue is not speed, or parallelism, but the completeness of the rule base.

Assuming that an AI program is well constructed, won't parallel processing make it run faster? Perhaps. It is true that certain aspects of most AI programs are heavily parallel, and would probably lend themselves well to parallel hardware architectures. The *Intellect* natural language system, for instance, has a major element of parallelism that is currently simulated through a process known as recursion. However, this parallel element isn't a major consumer of the resources consumed by *Intellect*. If parallel computers become available, programs like *Intellect* could probably achieve some speed-up by running on them, but only the portion of the program amenable to parallel processing—perhaps 10 percent in *Intellect*'s case—could exploit the architecture of such machines.

Is it therefore necessary to tie AI development to that of parallel processing? If anything, such a linkage could prove disastrous if AI programs are developed in such a way that their useful operation *requires* parallel processing. It's important to understand that parallel processing is not a new concept. People have been working on this idea for decades, and there are probably close to 75 such research projects— most government funded—ongoing in the United States. So far, only very limited parallelism has appeared in the market. It's an extremely difficult concept to harness, and there's no certainty that Japan will succeed in doing so in the next several years. If they fail in that objective, and if their AI programs are too dependent upon parallel machines, where does that leave them? Pity the ICOT researchers whose charge is essentially: "We not only want you to solve these heretofore unsolvable AI problems, we also want you to solve them with a parallel machine, which no one has been able to get a handle on either."

A less risky approach is to continue AI development targeted toward the millions of computers already installed. They aren't going to disappear overnight, regardless of the progress of parallel computing. When parallel machines begin to appear on the market, AI researchers will be among the first to have access to them, and will perhaps be best able to exploit their power. Until then, it's perfectly legitimate, and probably preferable, to have the government fund the two areas as two separate entities.

Of course, government support goes beyond funding. In Japan, the government plays a very active role as a matchmaker between different companies and between industry and the universities. The opposite has been true in the United States until recently. Here, the federal role was not to match firms, but to keep them separate. If anything, its role in working with universities was to ensure that the schools weren't heavily dependent upon industrial support. Strong concerns exist about close partnerships between industry and universities, with many fearing that the corporate world will inappropriately influence the focus of the academic environment.

These restrictions and attitudes are beginning to change. In the educational realm, the government is looking with more favor on industrial/university liaisons, in part because the universities themselves have started to realize that, with proper controls, such partnerships can prove extremely beneficial to their students. And in the antitrust world, the federal government has become more willing to permit the formation of consortiums and joint projects between competitors. If anything has facilitated this relaxation, it's the belief that the United States must respond in kind to the Japanese cooperative models. In the computer and AI arena, the new attitude has permitted the formation of what may be a major factor in the future market—the Microelectronics and Computer Technology Corp., or MCC.

A Consortium of Competitors

MCC, based in Austin, Texas, began operations in January 1983. The brainchild of Control Data Corp.'s former chairman William C. Norris, MCC is commonly presented as America's answer to the Japanese threat in computers and AI. MCC defines itself as "a private sector joint research and development venture created to help maintain U.S. technological preeminence and international competitiveness in microelectronics and computers." Its literature talks of the need to help U.S. firms "meet the challenge from government-supported R&D programs that have allowed firms in Japan and Western Europe to target U.S. industries."

The consortium has about 15 members, or shareholders, who pay for one share of "stock" in the organization. The members include Advanced Micro Devices, Allied, BMC Industries, Control Data, Digital Equipment, Harris, Honeywell, Martin Marietta Aerospace, Mostek,

Motorola, National Semiconductor, NCR, RCA, Rockwell, and Sperry. Notably absent from the list is IBM, which reportedly feared that its participation could have a negative impact on the venture. MCC has already raised antitrust sentiment in some quarters, and that sentiment could become a major factor should IBM become a consortium member, or so the story goes.

Initially, an MCC share cost $150,000, but it has already escalated to over $250,000. MCC has formed an associates program for smaller firms unable to meet the high cost of full sponsorship. Charged on a sliding scale based on total corporate revenues and purchases related to computers and microcircuits, the associates are given nonproprietary technical reports and newsletters and can participate in MCC's research symposia.

Aside from the membership fee, MCC's sponsors must contribute funding for one of the consortium's four main research programs. This funding reportedly ranges from $1 million to $4 million per year per program; several of the participants have invested in all four tracks. These tracks are: semiconductor packaging, software technology, VLSI/ computer-aided design, and advanced computer architecture. This last category is the most ambitious, and is the one most involved with AI. It consists of four subprograms: parallel processing, database system management, human factors technology, and artificial intelligence/ knowledge-based systems.

The MCC participants must agree to fund at least one of the four main programs for a minimum of three years. MCC will hold title to all resulting knowledge and patents, and will license them to the programs' participants. The technologies will be licensed to outside companies after a three-year period. MCC's participants will receive approximately 70 percent of the resulting royalty income, with the remainder used to finance further MCC research.

Directing the MCC operation is Admiral Bobby Inman, whose long government career included a stint as head of the National Security Agency. Inman's many political connections, coupled with the general U.S. concern about Japanese competition, have helped smooth the path through Congress of legislation meant to ease the antitrust laws that might limit or outlaw MCC. The consortium and its member companies have also worked closely with the Justice Department, apprising it of MCC's activities and intentions. So far, the strategy seems to be working, helped along by the spectre of Japan.

Inman has also succeeded in obtaining enough private funding to make working at MCC an attractive option to staying at a computer company or a university. (MCC is keeping its distance from DARPA, preferring to rely upon funds from its members to maintain its independence.) MCC pays competitive salaries and it offers the potential for a 50 percent bonus if an employee achieves his or her designated research plan. This is meant to compete with the bonuses based on profitability that are common at many computer firms. Because MCC is a nonprofit research organization, it came up with its own innovative package.

Even with its competitive remuneration, MCC had a difficult time finding staff, especially in the AI field. According to its bylaws, MCC's shareholders are permitted one liaison person associated with each of the projects they fund. The liaisons keep the companies informed about the ongoing research and transmit company suggestions about the direction of the research. Beyond the guaranteed liaison positions, each member company can propose its own employees for MCC positions, but the consortium is under no obligation to hire from the ranks of its members.

In fact, MCC was forced to radically modify its initial plans to staff up almost totally with researchers on temporary leave from the member firms. It seems that contributing money to the MCC venture was a lot easier than lending it scarce personnel—a problem that has also plagued Japan's ICOT. Inman was so disappointed in the quality of researchers the sponsors first sent to MCC that he began a vigorous policy of direct hiring the best talent he could find, regardless of the source. "I got assurances that all the talent we needed could be found in the shareholder companies," Inman said. "But when the time came to assemble it, the quality of talent we needed just did not materialize" (*High Technology*, 10/85).

Only after the member firms realized that the consortium could end up running with virtually none of their staff present did they begin to send quality people to Austin. At last count, about 65 percent of

140   ARTIFICIAL INTELLIGENCE ENTERS THE MARKETPLACE

MCC's staff consisted of direct hires, with the remainder coming from sponsor companies.

Handicapping MCC's Prospects

While it's reasonable to view MCC as our most direct counterbalance to Japan's triumvirate, we can hardly be assured of the consortium's success. For one thing, Japan has a lot more experience than the United States with such cooperative ventures. We know from the past that if ICOT manages to come up with some good ideas, the Japanese computer firms will be able to translate them into commercial products. We can assume that MCC researchers will also have good ideas, but getting them into the market will be no easy task. Even companies with long experience in turning technological ideas into products often let good ideas die in their labs. Probably the most notable example of this is Xerox's Palo Alto Research Center. PARC pioneered technologies ranging from computerized workstations to advanced graphics techniques only to let them languish until they were capitalized on by other firms.

Like most large corporations, MCC is unlikely to be able to move as quickly as smaller companies to incorporate new technologies into products. The successful small companies have always prospered by being like small fast boats that can outmaneuver the large corporate ships. So far, we're not even certain that the MCC ship can steer. If it can, it still has some major obstacles to clear.

The most dangerous of these is the consortium's distance from the ultimate consumer of its technology. For all computer development, but particularly with AI, there's got to be a very solid feedback cycle between the customers and the developers. When a researcher comes up with an idea, that's simply not the end of the process. The idea must be implemented at least in a prototype product so some customers can try using it. That use invariably raises a whole second class of problems the researcher never considered. In AI, it often takes four or five prototype generations before a company reaches the stage where it has a product acceptable to its customers.

Without such constant and detailed customer input, it's virtually impossible to gain the necessary experience with, and understanding of, the market. Such a feedback cycle is missing from the MCC paradigm. It's almost as if MCC hopes to develop a generic technology in an ivory tower and then give it to the member firms, saying, "Here it is. Now go out and do something with it."

In AI, the first cut is guaranteed not to work. Where does that leave MCC and its sponsors? Basically with the hope that people in the companies can understand the technology and do the next several levels of refinement. That's a big hope. The long AI development cycles require people who are committed to seeing the project through. If no such people exist, it won't get done. In MCC, the researcher who developed the idea, and may be the most committed to its commercial success, isn't likely to have much control over the technology's prospects once it leaves the lab.

Another hurdle MCC must overcome is the difficulty in developing technologies without having a clear target machine or computer environment at which to aim. Every vendor has its own "philosophy" of hardware and software design, and each develops new products internally with the goal of being consistent with that philosophy. Having such guidelines makes the development of new technologies much simpler than the development of generic technologies that can be adapted to a range of hardware with an equal degree of ease. Suppose an MCC research team has members from five sponsor companies. If each company sent off its respective researcher with the charge to "make sure you come up with something that will work well in our environment," some major problems will ensue. With all wanting to ensure that the approach is philosophically consistent with that of their own companies, the cooperative gains sought through the consortium model could quickly become dissipated.

Assuming MCC deals successfully with its internal R&D, its hands are tied when it comes to the commercial realization of any technology it produces. By law, the consortium can only develop technology to a prototype stage; it is prohibited from any product manufacturing or marketing. These tasks—those at which the Japanese excel—fall on the shoulders of the MCC sponsor firms and are a source of concern for

Inman. "The one part of this experiment that worries me is that we might end up producing the enabling technologies two years before Japan," Inman has said. "But unless the [MCC sponsors] are far swifter at taking that technology to the marketplace than U.S. companies have been in the past, they may end up finding Japanese products getting to the market in the same timeframe" (*High Technology,* 10/85).

Given these problems, MCC's ability to achieve major success is at least open to question. Nevertheless, the consortium model is a necessary component of this country's AI resources. Realistically, MCC will come up with some good ideas and some of its members will be able to take advantage of them. But to cast MCC as our primary answer to Japan's Fifth Generation discredits the proven ability of American computer companies, large and small, to set the computer evolution's rapid pace. And these companies aren't sitting back complacently watching Japan take the initiative in the crucial area of artificial intelligence.

The Entrepreneurial Lure

It is well known and documented that much of this country's technological innovation has originated in small firms. The early stages of AI development hold true to this pattern. While university and large corporate research departments must receive credit for breaking the theoretical ground, the first products incorporating AI have appeared under the auspices of small entrepreneurial companies.

AI development isn't cheap, and probably one of this country's major assets is the presence of a venture capital community willing to fund promising entrepreneurs. Aside from providing financial backing, the venture capitalists bring a certain rigor to what are often seat-of-the-pants operations. To protect their investment as much as possible, the backers require the entrepreneur to really think out and produce sound business plans, development timetables, and marketing strategies. Without such assurances, few venture capitalists will support a business, regardless of how good its basic idea.

In this way, the venture capital community winnows out some of the less stable entrepreneurs and gives needed guidance to others. It's easy to believe that all a firm needs to do to attract funding is to place "AI" in its name, but most venture capitalists are sophisticated enough to look beyond the surface, and to force the entrepreneur to do likewise. If there's a downside to the venture capitalist scene, it's that most have very aggressive goals in terms of what they want to recoup from their investment. To a degree, that limits their interest to areas of explosive, not just average, growth, so a lot of solid ideas probably go unfunded because they don't offer the desired potential return on investment. Without venture capital, though, many entrepreneurs in the computer and AI fields would never have gotten off the ground, and neither would their innovative ideas.

Even though few would dispute the fact that entrepreneurs have already come up with some useful AI products, many question whether such a rag-tag group of start-up companies can effectively counterbalance Japan's coordinated effort. An analysis of what drives entrepreneurs and an understanding of what some entrepreneurial companies have achieved suggests that we shouldn't sell short their potential.

On a fundamental level, the driving force behind entrepreneurs is simple, and its power can't be discounted: if they don't work, they don't eat. Why leave the security of a corporate giant or a university laboratory to enter the uncertain world of high-tech start-ups? In the case of AI, it's especially useful to consider the university alternative, since many of those entering the commercial AI realm are arriving directly from university research programs.

Clearly, the potential for financial gain in the commercial world is a big lure, although with AI, the history of success is not all that encouraging. After 30 years and millions of dollars of funding, AI is only now making some progress in the market, and that progress is checkered. Even if the field's financial uncertainty counteracts its potential financial rewards, a comparison of the university alternative helps make clear why some are willing to make the transition from professor to businessperson.

Surprisingly, the tasks faced by the head of a university AI department are not that different from those faced by an entrepreneur. Both, first of all, must spend a large part of their time raising funds for their programs. The professor goes to the school administration and to government and corporate sponsors; the entrepreneur typically goes to venture capitalists and corporate sponsors. With funding, each must then recruit skilled personnel—professors to staff the department or employees to run the start-up business. Each must take their initial plans for the programs and develop them into workable entities. For the department that means developing a strong curriculum, for the company it means creating a useful product. Finally, each has to market the fruits of their labor and find buyers—students in one case, and customers in the other.

Faced with the prospect of doing essentially the same type of job for the next five years, how does a person choose a course of action? Most look at academia and say, "Well it's very secure and you remain aloof from all the grubby issues of having to cover your own survival." But that's really not true. To build a new university program, the person has to go searching with hand outstretched for money, must recruit employees, and has to sell the product as well. After all that work, especially if the person is in a nontenured position, there's no assurance of a continued future at the institution. The professor who does much of the work may not even be a part of the program, much less its director.

The entrepreneur, on the other hand, is regarded as the key figure in an ongoing enterprise. While a business plan is subject to scrutiny and modification by those funding the venture, such oversight doesn't compare to the typical bureaucracy in a university. The entrepreneur is paid, and can pay employees, at a rate comparable to the rest of the market. The AI department head and faculty are confined to a schoolwide salary structure that may bear no relation to the market value of the individual professor's skills.

With a long-term commitment so important to the success of any AI project, be it a school department or a commercial product, any sense that the success of the project is beyond the control of the main instigator can be devastating. In the same way that the MCC researchers may find it difficult to rely upon the sponsor companies to make good on developing the consortium's technologies, the university department head may have problems accepting the limitations of his or her power within the university environment. In the same way that university restrictions and commercial attractions have drawn numerous scientists from universities into the biotechnology industry, a migration of AI professors into entrepreneurial companies has been underway for some time.

A Risky Business

If entrepreneurial firms have been known for their technological innovation, they have also been known for their high rate of failure. In a business like AI, where many of the recruits are direct from the university realm, the risk of failure is increased. The very nature of AI development works against a start-up's success. With AI products, it's extremely hard to judge progress or to evaluate whether or not you're even on the right track. Unfortunately, entrepreneurs have little margin for error.

AI products demand a long and intensive development cycle. With any other technology, it's possible to look at the prototype and say, "It works," or "It meets the specifications." There are always bugs in big systems, but at some point in the development, the researcher can recognize that the essential product is there and that it will be marketable within a set period of time. That just doesn't happen with AI.

A natural language system, for instance, is never really "done." At least for the foreseeable future, no such system will be able to accept all English questions; at best, it will only be able to answer enough questions in a certain application to make it a useful tool for its users. How does the developer know when that point has been reached? Invariably, the needs of the market outstrip the developer's initial evaluation of what is necessary. The whole process is one of an asymptotic approach to a solution, rather than a situation where one has yet to reach the solution one day and then suddenly achieves it the next.

Because the demands on AI systems can escalate so rapidly in real market settings, even experienced businesspeople can be caught off guard. Far too often, when a developer believes an AI product is 90 percent complete, the market shows otherwise. If an entrepreneurial venture's existence depends on achieving a payback within a set period of time, the discovery that an expert system with 200 rules really needs 1000 rules to function adequately can spell disaster.

Large corporations such as IBM clearly have an advantage in this regard. They can support long development cycles and can withstand unanticipated setbacks. Such companies are so diversified that a single product is rarely crucial to their survival. They can afford many simultaneous development efforts, and if 98 out of 100 fail to produce marketable products, the two successful projects can usually be leveraged enough to justify the cost of the 98 dead ends. Even if an introduced product is found to be lacking, a company such as IBM has the luxury of reworking it to meet the customers' needs.

In an entrepreneurial situation, you've got one and only one choice. You go with it, you're right or wrong, and you're successful or not. If your product has flaws, this may be fatal. Even if the entrepreneur's instinct were right and the product proves useful, there is still the hard fight for recognition and the cornering of a small market niche.

On the bright side, the entrepreneurial firm is not without advantages over its corporate counterparts. Foremost of these is the ability to move quickly and decisively in the production of new products. The resulting enviable record of innovation has not gone unnoticed by the large corporations, nor by MCC. Many of these huge entities have attempted to cultivate pockets of entrepreneurial activity within their walls, and to some degree they've succeeded. A notable example was IBM's creation of a development team that was given virtually free rein to design a computer with which IBM could gain entry to the lucrative microcomputer market. Working out of Boca Raton, Florida, the independent team followed its instincts, which in some cases ran counter to IBM's standard operating procedures, to come up with the IBM Personal Computer. The product went on to rout all but a few of its competitors in the small business computer market, something that probably surprised IBM as much as anybody.

IBM didn't pioneer the personal computer market. That task fell upon entrepreneurial firms like MITS and Apple Computer. While the IBM PC was a huge market success, few considered the computer to be highly innovative. Most technical innovation has first appeared in the products of smaller companies. It then falls to the larger firms to follow the lead and, perhaps, to firmly establish the new technologies in the marketplace.

Why is it difficult for a company like IBM to be the first on the market with new technologies? It's certainly not due to a lack of talent. IBM's labs probably have as great a concentration of skilled and resourceful innovators as any other research center, but the constraints imposed by the company's size and, ironically, its dominant position in the world of computers, can keep new technologies bottled up in the lab for inordinate amounts of time.

The main reason for this is simply because IBM has such a huge and broad customer base that no problem is simple to solve. Because it has to consider its existing base when developing new products, IBM may have to solve a problem for thousands of environments, not just one. Smaller firms can come out with solutions that answer the needs of 10 percent of the market, but IBM can't afford to do that. Its solutions have to be good for virtually everybody. This makes even simple problems hard to solve, and hard problems like those encountered in AI can be staggeringly difficult to overcome.

Also, because its potential market for new technologies is so huge, IBM has to consider carefully the prospects of supporting products incorporating the technology. It's fair to expect that such products may be around for 10 years or so before becoming totally obsolete, and the ramifications of that tenure can be very complex for a firm such as IBM. Added to all this is the very real desire on the part of any big computer vendor not to introduce a new technology that obsoletes its existing product line too soon.

This last consideration is clearly of no matter to the start-up entrepreneur. If anything, the entrepreneur *hopes* to retire existing products by the strength of a new technology. Realistically, the entrepreneur can't expect to seriously threaten the installed base of a giant like IBM or even those of second-tier firms such as Digital Equipment or Hewlett-Packard. But a start-up firm can prosper and grow if it succeeds in attracting even a tiny percentage of the larger firms' customers into its fold. Eventually, if the start-up grows large enough, or if a large number of such firms keep nibbling away at the big companies' markets, the major players will jump into the new business themselves.

A classic example of this scenario was played out over the past several years in the minicomputer market. Companies such as DEC, HP, and Data General had established large bases of dedicated users for their minicomputer products. Then, a few years ago, several small vendors started building computers based on powerful microprocessor chips. The mass-produced chips were inexpensive and a single chip could perform the same function that hundreds of separate components performed in a minicomputer. The minicomputer vendors were suddenly faced with low-cost "supermicro" systems that equalled or surpassed the performance of the more-traditional machines. After a couple of years of losing market share to the upstart supermicro vendors, the minicomputer firms finally responded with microcomputer products of their own. In the process, they managed to crush some of the pesky small firms, but a number have survived and prospered. Without the supermicro entrepreneurs forcing the issue early on, the arrival of the useful technology they championed would have been long delayed.

The situation is likely to be repeated with AI, although AI is just as likely to create new markets as it is to obsolete old ones. Although many of the major computer firms have long researched AI technology, the first to market with actual products were the small entrepreneurs. In this instance, the very visible Japanese effort will probably stimulate a large-company response as much as the entrepreneurs' early products, but so far it's been the entrepreneurs, not the Japanese, who have set the commercial AI pace.

Finally, with regard to the ability of entrepreneurs to counter the Japanese project, it's easy to forget that successful small firms can quickly become influential large corporations in the computer industry. Such establishment companies as DEC, HP, Data General, and Intel were tiny start-ups not long ago. They all managed to profoundly influence the world market and they continue to compete effectively in it. A more familiar example of such success is that of Apple Computer, which less than a decade ago was the proverbial two-man operation working out of a garage. Today, Apple's personal computers offer the only major competition to the IBM PC, and they continue to set the trend for much personal computer technology. All this in a market Japan's corporate giants have been unable to crack. Who's to say an AI entrepreneurial firm won't be able to achieve the same success?

Educational Shortcomings

If we can take some comfort in the thought that the combination of our entrepreneurial firms, our corporate giants, and our MCC consortium should be up to the Japanese challenge, we can't be so smug about the state of our educational system. Often, it's the Japanese universities that are presented as a liability to that country, accused of being unable to cultivate innovation in their charges. This third leg of the Japanese triumvirate reflects the mores of the country's homogeneous society, it is said, teaching its students to conform rather than to challenge.

Whether that's true or false, it's difficult to estimate how it will affect the Fifth-Generation Project's success. As we've seen, a single individual can be the genesis of revolutionary change, and it would be foolish to assume that ICOT has been unable to assemble individuals with such potential. Meanwhile, the U.S. university system, so esteemed by most, has its own share of problems. They pertain to the computer area in general, and to the AI field in particular. Few people realize how far removed our computer educational system is from the needs and the activities of the business world.

This is not to say that businesses should be unduly able to influence the curricula in universities. The schools shouldn't have to narrow the focus of their programs just to meet the demands of industry. But it's hard to argue against there being some similarity between what industry needs and what students should learn. After all, the students are the schools' customers, and the schools owe it to their students to provide them with an education that is current for that point in history, not one that is dated by 10 years. In the computer field, few schools are up with the times.

We have already detailed the evolution of computer languages. You have to look hard, however, to find examples of universities teaching fourth-, much less fifth-, generation programming. Nearly all computer science curricula are based solely on third-generation languages. While the importance of these languages cannot be questioned, they are clearly not an appropriate tool for all students. Most students will never find the need to program in BASIC, FORTRAN, or Pascal. Their use of the computer will likely be through spreadsheets, fourth-generation languages, or database packages. Each of these systems present their own approach, or "metaphor," for programming. These are approaches that for most students are far more relevant than third-generation languages. But, by and large, our universities are not teaching them.

They are not being taught for two reasons. First, most universities have an aversion to teaching the use of proprietary commercial products. They are much more comfortable using generic languages. Unfortunately, the new approaches to programming are only available as commercial products. Second, the gap between the academic world of computer science and the commercial use of computers is enormous. Amazingly enough, it is still possible to encounter professors of computer science who don't really understand what a spreadsheet is! The failure to include these paradigms in the educational program comes not from a reasoned analysis, but from failure to keep abreast of the rapidly changing commercial sector.

Keeping up with the state of the art in computer science can be a daunting task, but the effort has to be made if we are to have any hope of preparing our graduates to move smoothly into modern industry. All too often, professors express the following attitude: "We can't teach every little change that appears in the commercial world. The changes just come and go too quickly. Because of this we have to distill out the fundamental theoretical concepts and teach those, because those concepts will transcend any particular fad."

For this approach to succeed the professors must be able to separate out the field's true evolution from its transient fads, and few have managed to make this distinction. As a result, many of the programmers we're training must learn a new kind of programming at their first jobs.

For the students who do become programmers, there is another aspect of programming that they must learn on the job because the universities don't teach it. This is the methodology for large system's design and its impact on maintenance. These are two of the most critical aspects of a programmer's skill, but they are not usually taught at universities because the time constraints of an academic semester restrict assignments to a sequence of very short programs. These short assignments cannot have sufficient complexity to illustrate the importance of a design methodology.

Furthermore, the assignments are thrown away immediately after submission. The student is not required to maintain the program over a period of time. For this reason, the student never gets a chance to "feel the pain" caused by earlier design flaws. Both of these skills could be taught in a college programming course by building on a sequence of assignments during the term to tackle a difficult problem. Unfortunately, the isolation of the academic community is such that the professors themselves have not had sufficient experience in this arena to realize the importance of these issues.

With such fundamental problems present in even traditional computer science curricula, it's no wonder that there's a dearth of graduates competently trained in AI. Aside from a few major universities such as MIT, Stanford, and Carnegie-Mellon, few schools are thought to have high-quality AI programs. If we accept the fact that artificial intelligence has the potential to effect massive change throughout both the computer industry and our society, it seems obvious that more schools will have to devote more attention to keeping up with the times.

To succeed in this effort, a number of issues must be addressed. Schools clearly have a difficult time retaining good staff and attracting new professors in areas such as AI, where the commercial lures are so strong. Given the shortage of trained AI personnel, it's not surprising that the universities often come out on the short end of the hiring stick, and, consequently, have problems keeping current with industry trends.

While the migration to industry will probably strain the resources of universities in the near term, it's basically a good trend. Without the willingness of AI researchers to apply their knowledge in the building of products, the United States' commercial standing in the world of computers and AI would suffer. In the long run, the creation of a solid and productive commercial AI community will entice more students into the field. Over time, this will result in more trained AI personnel becoming available to meet both commercial and academic needs.

8

Near-Term AI

- Illegitimate AI Claims

- Unneeded AI Products

- AI on Personal Computers

- The Next Five Years

- Build Your Own

- Conversing with Computers

- Computer-Assisted Instruction

- Speech Recognition and Vision

Artificial intelligence didn't stay hidden in research laboratories for close to 30 years without reason. The technology has proven an extremely difficult one to commercialize, and it's safe to assume that this will remain so for some time. While some of AI's basic techniques are readily understandable, employing these techniques to shape useful products requires years of work based on accurate insights about market needs. The importance of the insights can't be trivialized, and the work can't be abbreviated. Unfortunately, a number of companies are trying to capitalize on the glamour of AI by building technological solutions for problems that don't exist, or by attempting to shortcut the necessary development time that is critical for any AI product. At the same time, there are a growing number of companies willing and able to work with AI on its own harsh terms.

In a world grown accustomed to constant hype about the fast blistering pace of the computer's evolution, the AI advances likely to occur in the near term may seem comparatively slow. It's important to recognize the distinctions between AI development and some of the computer revolutions that have astounded us over the past few decades. Many of these have been largely in the provinces of engineering and physics.

Computer engineers have progressively made the machines faster and more powerful, but these scientists have been working with well-understood physical properties. Electrons flow only so fast in certain materials, microscopic circuits can be shrunk only so small before one circuit begins to interfere with another, and circuit boards can be packed only so densely before the heat they generate melts them down. Scientists have pushed to the physical limits in all these areas, prompting the growing attention being focused on parallel computers that can increase power through the use of multiple processors.

Work in parallel processing hasn't progressed as quickly as that in single-processor computers, however. Why not? Because the well-understood physical constraints are of less importance here than are the difficult problems associated with programming parallel machines. Our brains routinely perform many parallel operations simultaneously, but how can we design computers that efficiently divide up complex problems among several processors? Which processors do which tasks, when do they perform them, and how do the various processors keep their neighbors informed about what they're doing? The solutions to these questions aren't readily apparent from anything we've learned about the physical world.

In the same way, the problems addressed by artificial intelligence require the breaking of new conceptual ground. Designers of computers that understand a wide range of English statements or that give expert advice about medical problems don't have much of a history on which to build. The fifth-generation languages of AI *are* part of a steady continuum within the evolution of programming, but the *applications* addressed by these programming techniques are totally new. They have no guideposts by which to advance; rather the guideposts are being constructed today through the trial-and-error progress of the AI entrepreneurs.

Illegitimate AI Claims

Given that there's no agreement as to what, exactly, the term "artificial intelligence" encompasses, it's impossible to draw a hard line between products that incorporate AI and those that don't. In a way, the distinction is moot. As with any computer product, the value to the user has nothing to do with the underlying techniques used to create the product. The user just wants something to solve a problem, and a product either solves it or doesn't. If it does answer a need, the product must be judged in its effectiveness against other products that solve the same need.

While all this seems obvious enough, it's in this regard—what problems are solved—that one can begin to judge the legitimacy of products that claim to use AI techniques. That is, a true AI product is likely to solve problems that have never before been addressed by computers. Payroll systems or word processors that claim to be AI based should be regarded with some skepticism. On the other hand, natural language systems, expert systems, and computers that learn probably do employ some AI methods. Of course, how well such systems work is an entirely different matter.

There's nothing inherent in AI programming that makes products based on it "good" products. Just as a bad COBOL programmer can botch a payroll system, so can a bad AI programmer produce a worthless expert system. The quality of the AI in a product is more important than its simple presence, and the way to judge this quality is no different from the way to evaluate any computer product: try it out. As we've noted, customers are better able to put a product through its paces than AI developers, who can never anticipate all a customer's demands. AI products that seem to function flawlessly in canned demonstrations built around their strengths have an alarming tendency to fall to pieces when called upon to perform in real application settings.

Evaluating the worthiness of "AI" products will probably be made more confusing by the fact that not all such products will really be based on AI. Already, the market is being inundated with vendor claims about the AI content of products that, by any objective assessment, incorporate only conventional computer technology. "Artificial intelligence" seems destined to go the way of such other misused labels as "user friendly" or "integrated." Once the market catches on to the terms, every product suddenly claims to incorporate them, justifiably or not. In fact, an interesting paradox has begun to occur. Because some vendors are starting to misrepresent their products, hoping to capitalize on the market's naivete about AI, some legitimate AI companies are starting to play down the AI content of their products. These companies rightly fear that the misleading claims of the AI pretenders may once again give the technology a bad name.

True AI developers are also in danger of alienating the market themselves. Failing to heed the lessons of the past, some firms are over-promising the technology, just as was the case for machine translation. When that technology couldn't meet its proponents' claims in the 1960s, AI was forced into a long period of disrepute and ostracism. Many fear that this cycle may soon repeat itself if some of the more outlandish AI claims take hold. When the products fail to back up these claims, the whole field may suffer. This will happen despite the fact that AI has already made, and will continue to make, many impressive advances in the power of computers.

Let's not forget the role of the press in setting up unrealistic expectations for AI. All too often, reporters and editors overlook the real advances being made by AI and instead concentrate on highly dubious futuristic scenarios for the technology. Sure, it's fun to read about household robots that serve drinks and vacuum the carpet, and it's frightening to contemplate the replacement of people by thinking machines, but we won't be living in a Buck Rogers world for a long time.

Nevertheless, such crystal-balling makes good copy, whereas objective analyses of the strengths and the limitations in today's AI technology may not. Ironically, the public may be so primed for truly incredible feats from computers of the future that the quantum leaps now being achieved by natural language and expert systems may seem comparatively insignificant. Science fiction, marketing hype, and blue-sky press reports about AI in the year 2010 are creating a population jaded to technological advances that, if judged by today's standards, would be seen to be truly amazing.

Unneeded AI Products

A curious aspect of much of the far-out AI speculation is that the envisioned products are often not something many people would want, regardless of their feasibility. There are companies today intent on producing the household robot of the future, but how many households will be willing to spend several thousand dollars for such an assistant? Today's rudimentary "personal" robots already cost that much, and they're little more than conversation pieces. As with every other computer technology, prices for personal robots will drop, but the cost of a robot actually able to understand natural language commands, see and interpret scenes, and perform a range of household tasks—all capabilities still far in the future—will be substantial. Is there really a large pent-up demand for such expensive mechanical servants?

We needn't look only to personal robots to find questionable applications for artificial intelligence. Misguided AI products will abound in the natural language and expert-systems areas also, because developers will ignore the dictum of only creating products that solve people's problems. Already, AI products are being built that are impressive technically, but unneeded commercially. Until AI developers break away from the mentality of simply looking for interesting technical riddles to crack, we're doomed to suffer through generations of sophisticated, but useless, products. The self-evident truth that it's better to discern the users' needs prior to building the products always seems to escape some practitioners.

There will be a number of useful, reasonably priced AI products, but the number will be limited for several years and the reasonable price will not be trivial. AI will follow the same route as most earlier computer technologies: the first implementations will be relatively expensive and built for larger computers for which high-priced software can be justified. The technology will then be scaled down to smaller computers, but the first versions of AI for lower-priced machines will lack the power and the complexity of their large-computer counterparts. Gradually, as AI becomes better understood and as the computers increase in power, the products available for personal computers will rival those designed for more expensive machines. At the same time, new AI breakthroughs will be appearing at the upper end of the market, and the filter-down cycle will continue.

What all this means is that sophisticated AI for the masses is still a distant ideal. Most people will get their first brush with artificial intelligence in the office using company computers. For some time, "AI" for home use will either not be real AI or will be very simple implementations of the technology. The AI products that do exhibit some reasonable degree of capability will enter the marketplace only haltingly, as a few customers initially prove the products' worth and others gradually follow their lead.

AI on Personal Computers

This prognosis may sound fairly gloomy, especially since much has been written lately about the striving of AI companies to bring AI software to personal computers. Indeed, a number of firms already sell natural language and expert systems that run on PCs. A crucial distinction must be drawn here. Namely, personal computers are not equivalent to home computers. Home computers are a subset of all personal computers, many of which serve in workplace environments. The most famous of these, the IBM Personal Computer, is too expensive for most home buyers, and has made its name in the corporate world.

In other words, developers *are* designing AI products for PCs, but almost always for business PCs. In offices, small computers can be linked together into networks, they can have access to expensive peripherals such as hard-disk storage and laser printers and, most importantly from the AI developer's view, they can make justifiable the purchase of software that would be far too expensive for the home personal computer user. Few home users would shell out $5000 or $10,000 for an expert-system accounting package, but many companies with PCs could easily justify such an expenditure. High-level AI implementations will likely cost at least that much for a number of years.

The AI vendor selling to anything other than the corporate market has some serious obstacles to overcome. To reach either the home or the small business market, the vendor is likely to rely upon retail store distribution of its products. However, the retail channel has become an increasingly hazardous sales route. The prices, and the resulting margins, a vendor can charge when selling through retail are considerably less than those possible if the product is sold direct to corporate users. As a result, only a few of the top-selling retail software products are turning a profit for their developers. To recoup the substantial development costs associated with any legitimate AI product, the vendor would have to sell an extremely large number of the products through the retail outlet. Plus the retail salespeople, not generally noted for their in-depth understanding of the products they sell, couldn't be counted on to give accurate or clear descriptions of an AI product's operation or of its application potential.

Even small business customers, who might seem a more attractive market than home-computer users, represent a problem area for AI vendors. Like the home-computer users, this group of users also buys largely through retail stores. While they can afford to spend more than home users, small businesspeople typically want to buy total solutions for their problems. AI is not yet in the business of providing complete solutions, nor are most entrepreneurial AI vendors capable of supplying the long-term hand-holding often necessary with small business customers.

It's easy to assume that the home and small business markets will be easy prey for vendors selling "AI" products that don't live up to the name. After all, these buyers are typically less sophisticated than buyers at large corporations, and the prices of lower-level products don't prompt as much prepurchase investigation as do $10,000+ software packages. So far, however, buyers at all levels of the market have shown some intelligence when confronted with AI claims. No blatantly false "AI" products have achieved much attention, and there's no reason to expect this to change. Changes can occur quickly in the personal computer market, but not so fast that a disreputable product can get too far before its flaws are revealed. This is even more true in the corporate computing environment, where any major change in technology can expect up to a 10-year waiting period from the time of its conception to the time that it achieves widespread acceptance in the market.

The Next Five Years

What form will artificial intelligence take in the near future? Various market analysts expect AI to be over a $2 billion industry by the end of the decade, so there will have to be some AI products around. Even

Business Week has trumpeted that "Artificial Intelligence Is Here." But where is here?

"Here" will be largely in the big corporations, in universities, and in the government, at least for the most-powerful implementations of AI. The government, through DARPA, will be working to produce various military AI systems. Many of the initial corporate systems will be proprietary products developed in-house by the corporations themselves. As long as two years ago, Digital Equipment Corp. estimated that more than half of the Fortune 1000 companies had established some kind of internal AI development group (*Computerworld*, 6/4/84). The object of some of these firms, of course, is to develop their own products for sale in the commercial realm. Others, however, hope to build expert and natural language systems to enhance their own operations, and will keep the technology proprietary in order to gain a competitive edge over their rivals.

Meanwhile, the number of established companies and start-up firms entering the AI field is already starting to mushroom. IBM has made some initial steps into the market, as have such companies as Digital Equipment, Texas Instruments, and Data General. New companies with names such as Teknowledge, Intellicorp, and Syntelligence have begun to establish a presence in the field. All are banking on AI becoming the hottest computer market on the horizon, and they're justified in that belief. Unlike some earlier computer technologies, AI won't have played all its cards within the first few years of its commercial existence. Through this decade, most AI products will be slowly pioneering new territory and providing a proving ground upon which later advances will build. No one has yet sighted the bottom of the AI well, and we can expect the technology to keep improving—often in areas we have no way of anticipating—throughout the course of our lifetimes.

The shape of things to come is already appearing in AI's early products. Most are relatively expensive and narrowly focused, but they can give some idea about the transformations AI will bring to computers. They demonstrate that, at least in its first tentative forays, artificial intelligence is indeed "here."

Build Your Own

If expert systems have taught us anything, it's that determining what expert help people need, and then building a relevant AI system can be a daunting job. A number of people confidently formed expert system start-ups after they had gained experience developing some of today's most famous AI prototypes. But the market quickly drove home the difficulties in moving from research prototypes to producing products that large numbers of people were willing to buy.

It turns out that it's no simple matter to identify broad markets in which expert systems can prove useful. Even if such applications can be discovered, it remains a back-breaking task to actually track down the necessary expertise and program it into a computer. The techniques for such knowledge acquisition and programming are still at a fairly rudimentary level.

We've already seen what many vendors have chosen as their answer to the barriers of building expert systems: let the customers build the systems themselves with the aid of the fifth-generation toolkits. The toolkit market really started to make headway in late 1984. The available kits range in power and price, with one costing only several hundred dollars and others surpassing $30,000. By definition, the toolkits don't help customers decide which problems to solve and they aren't magical programs that let nontechnical people build useful expert systems. The toolkits make life easier for sophisticated users who are willing and able to dirty their hands with programming, but the average consumer must wait for the products that the toolkits will help create.

Despite their notable lack of end-use functionality, the toolkits do represent an important step in the evolution of expert systems, as was illustrated in Chapter 5. Some of the first buyers of the toolkits have been other AI companies that plan to use them to build expert systems for resale. Some developers will continue to prefer to work with their own proprietary toolkits, but others will benefit from the ready availability of these products. As a result, we can expect to see a greater number of expert systems in a wider range of vertical applications than might otherwise have been the case.

There are some real expert systems entering the market. One early product reportedly helps bank officers evaluate the credit risk of loan applicants and is designed to run on a terminal connected to a large IBM computer. This system, like all near-term expert systems, is meant to directly assist its operators, not to operate autonomously. The system isn't even meant to be the higher authority in the human/machine partnership, but it does help ensure that the banker evaluating a loan prospect considers all the necessary factors. It even weighs the various factors and keeps track of the relative risks involved. Of course, the system can only evaluate the financial status of the prospect and place it in the context of the bank's lending policy. Although some of the questions it asks the banker are subjective, the system can't consider unanticipated factors that may be relevant to the loan consideration. For these factors, the banker must rely upon his or her own expertise.

Other recently announced expert systems include one that helps select the best customers to target in mass mailings, and another that assists financial consultants in evaluating and making recommendations to clients about personal investment strategies. The first is a mainframe-based software package that sells for $375,000 and is designed for use by large direct-mail marketeers and service bureaus. It evaluates the results of test mailings, looking for the mix of customer characteristics evident in those who respond to the direct-mail pitch.

The personal finance system comes bundled on a LISP machine and the whole package costs approximately $50,000. Its developers claim it has a knowledge base containing the equivalent of about 6000 rules, and also that it has a sophisticated report writer function that can automatically produce a detailed financial report for the client, charts and all. The vendor selling this product plans to keep a full-time subsidiary busy constantly updating the knowledge base to ensure that it remains current with such relevant issues as fluctuating tax laws and interest rates. The system user is also able to customize the expert system so that it follows rules specific to his or her investment-counseling strategy.

These examples are representative of how knowledge-based systems are likely to go. The products are designed for a narrow application, which makes the acquisition and programming of relevant rules feasible. Also, they rely to varying degrees on information and expertise provided by the users. Even if the banking system has some specific knowledge not known to the banker, it still needs the banker to make the final judgment about any loan. Few knowledge-based systems in the near future will be designed to work as autonomous experts, receiving, evaluating, and responding to data without the supervision of people.

The young expert system market is really beginning to develop. That can be seen by the fact that over 200 separate expert system projects were underway in Europe by late 1984 (*Datamation*, 11/1/84). These included a product that diagnoses and suggests treatment for agricultural diseases, a system that offers help in choosing which car to buy, and various systems designed to make different manufacturing processes more efficient and productive.

As in the United States, however, the Europeans are moving cautiously in their pursuit of expert systems. *Datamation* reported: "The European expert systems business . . . like its counterparts in the U.S. and Japan, still has to overcome a major credibility problem. Grandiose projects begun in the '70s suffered from a lack of understanding of both the technology and the tasks at hand. The resulting high costs, delays, and overzealous predictions of potential benefits by expert systems proponents have tempered user companies' enthusiasm for the technology."

Conversing with Computers

Natural language systems are the current AI success stories in the commercial realm. *Intellect*, the first such commercial system, is already used by several hundred of the nation's leading corporations. The impact that these systems are having on how information is disseminated within these organizations is quite profound. With *Intellect*, business professionals are able to use English queries to get at the vital corporate information base themselves. The mainframe computer market is now recognizing the benefits of natural language technology, as well as how it differs from, and relates to, other technologies such as database management systems and fourth-generation languages.

Unfortunately, "natural language" means many things to many people. Some vendors have taken advantage of this fact by sticking the "natural language" label on a wide variety of products, some AI-based, others not. A product's value isn't dependent on its AI content, but on its functionality. To some degree, of course, AI techniques give functionality beyond that otherwise obtainable, and buyers of a natural language system stand to be disappointed by the system's capabilities if it doesn't make some legitimate use of AI techniques.

The major difference between the various systems that purport to provide a natural language interface to a computer is the degree to which the products support flexibility and variation in the users' statements. On the low-end, some products merely give users lists of words that they can combine to form sentences that, because of the vocabulary restrictions, are guaranteed to be understood by the computer. Beyond that, some systems require the users to "train" them by entering commonly used phrases and describing the computer response each phrase should elicit. Some variation from the set phrases may be possible, but this flexibility is very limited. The computer essentially stores and recognizes the coded patterns of the words; it makes no attempt to analyze the statement's grammar or its conceptual content.

There are several natural language programs that do such sentence parsing and meaning analysis, but even here a wide range of capabilities exists. Some support only single definitions for words, which, as noted in Chapter 3, can be very limiting. The ability to deal with ambiguities is, after all, one of the fundamental skills involved in understanding natural language.

Many such limitations only surface through use of the system, and like all of AI, natural language has had only a short history from which to learn. Beyond that, the obvious factors of price and machine resources come into play. Clearly, a system designed to run on mainframe computers can be larger and more expensive than one meant for use on personal computers. The added size should permit the mainframe program to incorporate some additional features not feasible on a personal computer version, and the prices will reflect, in part, these differences. As experience grows, we can expect to see natural language systems equivalent to today's most powerful begin to become feasible on much smaller machines.

Computer-Assisted Instruction

Another area likely to see a growing influx of AI is that of computer-assisted instruction (CAI). Computers have served as teaching tools for years, often in such rudimentary applications as drill-and-practice spelling or math routines. The usefulness of CAI increased recently with the introduction of interactive videodisk technology. Most people equate this technology with that of video cassettes, upon which movies are distributed for home viewing. But in conjunction with a computer, the videodisk technology can permit students to see animated or real images and hear audio instructions in addition to computer-generated displays. Because the videodisks, unlike video cassettes, can be randomly accessed very quickly, the user can easily jump around to different sections of the instructional disk. Thus, the student can progress at his or her own pace, skipping material already known or repeating difficult lessons.

AI holds the promise of moving computer-assisted instruction to a new level of sophistication. The major goal sought through the inclusion of AI in teaching systems is the modeling of each individual student. In other words, through its interactions with the students, the computer would build a profile of each user, and would automatically tailor its lesson plan to suit the capabilities and interests of each student. In so doing, the computer would have to "learn" new information as it went along. Computer learning is crucial to numerous AI applications, but such a capability has yet to appear outside the walls of the research labs.

Simple versions of CAI systems have been around for some time, but it's often difficult to extend them beyond their low-level capabilities. For instance, in the late 1970s Dartmouth College had a computer system designed to help students understand how to write BASIC programs correctly. Students would write programs in answer to four problems the system understood, the programs would be run, and the teaching system would look at the answers and postulate where, if anyplace, the students made errors in writing the programs. Within its narrow domain, the system worked fairly well, and some Dartmouth faculty decided to obtain a grant to expand the system into a much broader-knowledge product. An investigation quickly showed that any upgrade of the product would be extremely complex, and the expected results weren't anything that would justify the effort or the expense. Once again, the leap from crude non-AI products to sophisticated AI solutions was shown to require a major commitment.

Some people point to any expert system as a potential candidate for educational purposes because such systems almost always have a feature that permits them to explain the logical steps they followed to arrive at a conclusion. This elucidation feature, some argue, could have instructional value to anyone not understanding a process that the expert system can perform. The caveat here is that, in order to get expert systems to work, the individual rules must be tiny and precise. As such, a listing of the steps the system followed to reach a conclusion may be totally arcane from a user's point of view. It's as if a person who didn't understand a geometry problem asked for an explanation and got a 50-line proof. The person may still not understand the gist of the proof simply because it's at the wrong level of detail to make much sense.

Given the current state of AI, it's probably unrealistic to expect an incredible amount of progress in AI-based computer-assisted instruction over the next few years. This isn't to say that CAI won't make dramatic advances during this time, just that few of the advances will have their roots in AI. More groundwork, especially in the area of computer learning, needs to be accomplished before we can expect computer assistants that come anywhere close to rivaling the talents of human instructors.

Speech Recognition and Vision

Two other areas often placed within AI's purview are those of speech recognition and computer vision. The first has a particularly close relationship with natural language processing, which so far depends upon commands typed via the computer keyboard. When speech recognition technology becomes more reliable and more cost effective, the technology could be easily grafted onto existing natural language products, permitting users to speak a variety of commands that the computer could understand. Simple implementations of such "speech understanding" systems will begin appearing within the next two years.

Without going into great technical detail, almost all speech recognition systems available today are "speaker-dependent, discrete-speech" systems. This means that each speaker must train the system to recognize his or her voice speaking individual words. Once the system is trained, the user must speak in a halting manner to ensure that discernable pauses exist between each word. Only slight progress has been made on "speaker-independent, continuous-speech" systems, and reasonably priced products of this type are still a number of years away.

Today's speech systems recognize a speaker's voice by storing voice patterns of the words in their vocabulary. When a word is spoken, the system compares the pattern it generates with those stored in its memory, looking for a match. If one is found, the system typically displays the word on its screen for confirmation by the speaker. If no match is made, the system will request that the speaker again say the word. The accuracy of different systems varies widely, with some being more susceptible than others in failing to recognize words spoken, say, by an authorized user who has a cold or who is too far from the computer's microphone.

Although speech recognition started firmly within the AI field, it has since broken somewhat away from its AI association. The pattern-recognition process it uses became so formalized and so mathematical that the people interested in speech recognition decided it would be best to disassociate their field from the more heuristic world of AI. In fact, some of the technical advances that are making speech recognition more feasible have no relation whatsoever to artificial intelligence. For example, the storage requirements of voice patterns can be staggering, and that has severely limited the size of vocabularies that the systems could support. Now that computer memory prices have dropped considerably, one of speech recognition's major barriers to success has effectively been overcome.

Other developments in speech recognition, however, are closely tied to AI. One prototype system, designed to understand 10,000 words and to have the capability to operate as a "voice-activated word processor," consists of a variety of "expert" modules that use different methods to identify spoken words. One module, for example, can disambiguate homonyms based on their context. The system also uses natural language parsing to show the parts of speech for each word and their relationships to one another. These techniques, combined with advanced acoustic resolution, have reportedly resulted in a recognition accuracy rate of over 97 percent in the experimental system.

Machine vision is more clearly in the realm of AI because it typically involves much more interpretation than speech recognition. A system that must view a scene via a TV camera and analyze that scene raises complex problems not usually encountered in speech. Machine vision has hundreds of potential uses, some of which, such as image analysis, are essentially static in nature. However, the most publicized applications involve applications such as robotics, in which the machine uses its "sight" to move itself and perhaps other objects within the frame of its vision.

One of the more common robot-vision problems is called "bin picking." In this application, the robot must view a group of objects randomly piled in a container and lift them out, one by one. Of course, the robot needs not only to see and identify the boundaries of the individual objects, but must also see where its own gripper is in relation to the desired part and move its arm accordingly. The computations involved in successfully completing this identification/movement/gripping/removal cycle are substantial. To make matters worse, the vision provided by most TV cameras is often inadequate for discerning an object's location in three-dimensional space. Some progress is being made, but few major advances are likely before the next decade.

To summarize, AI work is ongoing across many fronts, but all of it is in the formative stage of development. The rapid advances common in other areas of computer technology won't be repeated in AI because AI, more than the other sectors, requires the breaking of new conceptual ground. The technology *is* already available in a variety of forms, but generally in narrow domains in which the variables encountered are strictly limited. Through the end of the decade AI will become more widespread and begin to exert a noticeable impact in the workplace and on society in general, but the major advances envisioned by many won't be available commercially until the 1990s.

9

What the Future Holds

- Will Machines Really Think?
- The AI Landscape
- Generating New Knowledge
- Machines That Learn
- Knowledge of the Self
- The Curiosity to Know

No one has yet shown an ability to accurately predict the future of traditional computer science, and there's no reason to think that AI's future can be foretold with any greater accuracy. The 30-year history of modern computer science is littered with discarded predictions and projections that fell far from the mark of reality. Most of the early prognostications failed to anticipate the quantum leaps that computer hardware would make. The microprocessor chip, massive computer memories, and incredibly high-resolution displays were among the advances that caught most of the crystal-ballers sleeping. Availability of such devices has resulted in computers that are smaller and vastly more powerful than anyone could have foreseen 10 or 15 years ago.

The predictions weren't all on the short side. Probably the most notable error of optimism was the widespread belief in the mid-to-late 1970s that personal computers would be ubiquitous by the beginning of this decade. By the 1970s, people were getting accustomed to the rapid technical evolution of the computer field, and they mistakenly assumed that the mere existence of inexpensive processors would create massive markets for the machines. What the analysts overlooked was the need for software that would make the computers useful to small businesses and home users. Many who bought small computers soon discovered that they made good paperweights, and not much else. Eventually, the industry shook its blind obsession with hardware and began to devote more of its resources to the development of application software. With the personal computers finally able to perform some useful functions, the machines are beginning to spread through-out society. But this gradual movement is far behind the schedule laid out by some 10 years ago.

As with personal computers, AI seems destined to arrive more slowly than much of today's hype would have us believe. As with the computer field in general, AI's evolution will be moderated by both technological and market factors. At any given level of technology, the AI applications with the most potential for commercial leverage will be those first developed, and those applications will not necessarily be the most glamorous or esoteric of the bunch. Some firms will no doubt pursue the creation of personal robots, for instance, but the development of natural-language processing and knowledge-based systems for personal computers will receive far more attention and will have a far broader impact.

Will Machines Really Think?

Coincidental with AI's evolution will be the long-running philosophical debates about the feasibility of thinking machines and, if possible, their role in our world. These debates are subtly distinct from those concerning what functions AI-based computers will be likely to perform in the future. In other words, technologists will argue about what functions state-of-the-art machines will be able to do at any given time, and philosophers and the public at large will argue about whether these functions represent thought and reasoning.

While no shortage of differing opinions exists among the technologists about what operations AI-based computers will be able to perform, the fact is that actual demonstrations of capabilities will, sooner or later, prove some predictions wrong and others right. The resolution of the philosophical debates is less certain. Much of the disagreement here springs from the fact that there's no consensus about the meaning or the measurement of such concepts as "thinking" and "reasoning." As long as different definitions exist, so will different opinions about machines' ability to demonstrate these traits. By some definitions many of today's computers already reason and some might be said to think.

But if thinking is defined, *de facto*, as a characteristic of only a few forms of biological life, AI will never measure up to its requirements.

The philosophical argument is valuable because it causes people to more closely examine and evaluate their own mental processes, an introspection that is inherently difficult for most of us. Admittedly, some of this evaluation may be done in desperation, as people search for traits that distinguish them from AI machines. On a practical level, such distinctions will be easy to find for a long time. AI will do impressive things, but only in narrow domains of expertise or functionality. The day of a computer as multitalented and well-rounded as the average person is clearly a distant ideal.

The AI Landscape

Although AI is still a rarity in the world of computers, this will change dramatically. It's likely that almost all of the computers sold by the end of this century will rely upon AI to some degree or another. In the constant quest to make computers easier to use, successive generations of natural language processing will become staples on most machines. Before 1990, the long-awaited capability of speech recognition should be more readily available, and will begin interfacing to natural language software. Meanwhile, developers will have broadened AI applications beyond the current expert systems. A wide variety of inexpensive expert systems will likely be available within the next 10 years, and AI techniques will have been applied to other application areas such as entertainment and education.

As a side note, it's not certain that the term "artificial intelligence" will stay in vogue for all these future developments. If any phenomenon has proven common within the amorphous AI realm, it's that many research fields considered to be part of AI suddenly loose that association when the research begins to pay off in actual products. Paradoxically, it's as if "artificial intelligence" is meant to only describe some future, virtually unreachable functions; attaining the functions means they couldn't really be AI. It is possible, however, to be certain that the programming techniques associated with AI today, and the future techniques built on this fifth generation, will produce varieties of computers that would not have been possible without a foundation in what we now call artificial intelligence.

With AI, or its descendants, destined to be so ubiquitous, we can safely assume that the impact of computers in and on our society will be greatly magnified in the coming years. It's fair to expect that most homes will have computers, as will most offices and most classrooms. This pervasiveness will result largely because AI techniques will have made the machines more valuable and easier to use. The sheer presence and availability of so many computers is bound to reshape many of our activities and attitudes.

Our society will become one in which access to sources of knowledge and information is both simple and increasingly important. The trend toward this state of affairs is not new. Even before the first computers came onto the scene, information was recognized as a valuable, if intangible asset; thanks to computers, it has achieved the aspects of a commodity. AI will make this commodity cheaper and available to more people, and will also help add to the storehouse of known information. Who will best use this packaged information and how its exploitation will affect our overall society is impossible to predict.

The very existence of computerized knowledge of all sorts has some general implications, however. The scope of these implications can be evaluated in part by considering how the widespread availability of books affected civilization. With Gutenberg's invention of movable type for printing presses, information and knowledge that had been limited to an elite few was made available to many throughout society. Of course, being able to exploit books first required that people could read, a talent not particularly useful in the absence of printed books. Books, therefore, not only made information available to a wider audience, they motivated that audience to improve their own reading talents in order to access the information. The combined, snowballing effect of disseminating more knowledge throughout society and the growing capacity of the population to understand this knowledge has been staggering. In all fields of endeavor, from the arts and humanities to the sciences, the ability to share information with an increasingly literate populace has had incalculable benefits.

For all their power, books have a severe limitation. The information they contain is static. You can't ask a book questions, you can't add information to it, and you can't even apply its information directly to specific problems unless its author happened to anticipate your exact need. This shortcoming is exacerbated by the levels of transfer involved in disseminating information in the printed form. An author takes some ideas and puts them in a very linear form for storage. Several years later a person picks up the book, reads it, tries to deal with any ambiguities, builds an intellectual model of what the author is trying to impart, which may or may not mirror what was in the author's head, and then tries to interpret and use the information.

A good example of how ineffective this whole process can sometimes be is in the area of "how to" books. Say a person who knows how to play a little chess buys a chess strategy book with the intent of improving his game. Typically, in such a situation, the person's ability will actually get worse immediately after reading the book. Why? The reader already had a cohesive theory about how to play. Perhaps it wasn't optimal, but at least the user had experience with it. The book will have taught the reader a few new things, but somehow the new information clashes with the old theory. The result is that the reader is weaker in certain areas until the new information can be assimilated with the old. This process of assimilation relies upon the reader's own ability to gradually make mental connections between the disparate information in order to build a new, integrated theory. The static book can't be said to offer much help in this integration.

Say, instead of a chess book, the player had access to Bobby Fischer's theory of play implemented on an AI system. The player could ask the system questions, give it specific problems, and get advice specific to those problems. But most importantly, the user could ask the system, "Why?" There's no quantitative proof that this arrangement would be an improved way to communicate chess theory, but, intuitively, one suspects it would hold great potential. It's closer to the paradigm of having an individual instructor work with an individual student, which most of us would agree is a more efficient method of transferring information than having the student just read a book. Of course, books contain detail that may surpass the teacher's knowledge, and books are certainly more readily available than instructors. AI might provide a vehicle that combines the exhaustive detail of books and the personal touch of instructors. Lest teachers surmise that such AI systems represent a threat to their job security, it's important to note that these dynamic sources of information will hardly be so powerful that they could replace human instructors. Rather, the AI systems might simply be more effective tools than books in some areas of endeavor.

It's even possible to envision AI-based novels that let the reader take a much more active role in interaction with the story. A simple representation of this concept are the adventure games already available that generate different sequences of events based on the choices made by the player, who acts as the main participant in the fantasy adventure. Someday it will probably be possible to create interactive storylines of a much grander and more detailed variety. The computer-based story would contain massive amounts of information about each character's personality and motivations, about different locations and about hundreds of other aspects integral to the specific tale. As with today's adventure games, the reader would act as a character in the story, and would influence its direction and its outcome depending upon which choices he or she makes while progressing through it.

Such an interactive "book," of course, would serve a different purpose than a novel. The novelist has a particular viewpoint of the world and uses the tools of the craft to communicate that viewpoint as effectively as possible to the reader. The interactive story serves a different purpose, and will initially be directed at providing more entertainment than enlightenment. However, it's conceivable that serious authors may someday be able to use this form to communicate not only their own perspectives, but also to cause readers to generate insights specific to themselves.

Generating New Knowledge

As important as it is, the fact that AI systems probably increase and improve the flow of information among people represents just one of the likely impacts of these machines. Beyond this role, AI should eventually make additions to the total reservoir of human knowledge. Evidence exists that some AI machines already have used their programmed rules and knowledge independently arrive at unique conclusions. So far, the tentative examples of such talent mostly involve esoteric mathematical insights and the proofs to support them. Nevertheless, we can reasonably expect that properly programmed machines will produce a wide range of information that has yet to be discovered by people.

As an example, take economics, which is often called more of an art than a science by both its practitioners and its detractors. Because there are so many variables in a model of the overall economic scene, it's extremely difficult for economists to develop hard scientific theories that accurately describe the fluctuations of the market and predict how changing one element of an economy will affect the total economic picture. There are so many factors to consider in both the micro- and the macroeconomic worlds that few if any people can hope to assimilate all the relevant information and devise theories as to how the pieces fit together.

Of course, economists already use computers extensively to run "econometric" models of the economy. These models are statistical in nature and rely upon abstract numerical formulas and masses of numbers to produce answers to questions. Aside from the fact that the answers are routinely unreliable, this numerical optimization kind of approach has another failing: It doesn't form a theory about the world it is analyzing. Such systems are inherently less interesting because, like a numeric solution to an algebra problem, the econometric models just give answers—right or wrong—to certain problems. The systems don't explain anything or create any theories or impart any understanding.

The AI approach, by contrast, is to give symbolic form to the problem. Cause and effect relationships would be embedded in the system as rules. As with an analytic solution to an algebra problem that gives an equation to solve the problem for all time or for all values, the AI system would codify the known information and put it in a form that is intelligible and consumable.

Suppose that a computer was programmed with all relevant facts about economics and the rules that describe the relationships between the facts. Such a computer would not only need AI programming techniques, but would also have to be a massively powerful machine. The technology to build such an economic expert system is not that distant. Would such a system be able to discern fundamental truths about economics that have so far escaped even the best economists? No one can say, but many would like to find out. Economics is just one of hundreds of fields that could potentially benefit from such explorations.

Should some future expert system succeed in furthering our understanding of the dynamics involved with economic variables, would the society at large, or economists in particular, condemn the new knowledge just because it came from a machine? Of course not. If we suddenly gain new insight about how to better manage our economy, who's going to quibble over the source of the information? All science consists of a probing of the darkness, and AI-based machines will be welcome tools that shed some light across a wide variety of areas. The knowledge thus gained will not be somehow tainted or less true simply because it comes from a machine rather than from a human brain.

Machines That Learn

It's one thing to feed a computer a series of related rules and facts and have it derive new insights about the material; it's quite another thing to have a computer that learns new rules and facts on its own. The area of computer learning is one of the most fascinating and promising fields of AI. The methods employed today in the pursuit of machine learning are still rudimentary, but they will be substantially refined over the years. Whether machines have yet learned new material is a difficult question to answer, because it's hard to determine how the developer's bias might have inadvertently lead the machine to less-than-independent knowledge.

As an example of how machines might learn, consider a computer that can infer the grammar, or production rules, for a language by examining correct and incorrect examples of the language. Much as a child learns from positive and negative feedback, the computer would be shown hundreds of sentences with some labeled as being correct and others labeled as being wrong. Eventually, if properly programmed, the computer could infer from the examples a grammar that would accurately represent the structure of the language. In other words, the systems would be working backward from the normal scheme of things, in which it is first fed the rules and then asked to apply them to language understanding.

As we know, the structure of a language changes so slowly that it makes more sense to program the rules into the computer rather than giving it the ability to discern the rules itself. Other uses for this learning paradigm are easy to imagine. Take an expert system that is able to examine case studies of medical diagnoses, treatments, and results: Here a patient had certain symptoms, received a certain treatment, and recovered. Here a patient with similar symptoms received a different treatment and died. By examining volumes of such cases, the computer might be able to derive an inference mechanism for how to make diagnoses and how to suggest treatments. Medicine evolves more quickly than language, and as new knowledge is gained it could be added to the computer's storehouse, serving to automatically modify the computer's perspective about its area of expertise.

Once we have computers that can learn, doesn't that imply that the time of machine superiority is near? What's to stop these mechanical students from sucking in all the world's knowledge, producing more, and leaving human intellectual capabilities behind in the dust? For one thing, hardware limitations do exist. Even an intelligent, learning computer can only acquire that amount of information that fills its available memory space. And the word "acquire" still means spoon-fed by people.

Both these limitations will eventually become minor restraints. Employing new storage techniques such as optical laser disks and linking multiple computers and their memories together in giant communications networks could produce memory spaces that make the hundreds of millions of characters stored on today's large computers seem minuscule by comparison. Various branches of AI are already beginning to give computers senses such as vision and hearing with which they will be able to acquire new information without direct human support. But another barrier on the path to unlimited computer learning will be more difficult to overcome.

That barrier is the breadth and scope of knowledge initially given the computer. That is, a computer designed to study medical case histories and infer certain information from them simply doesn't have the range of rules to make inferences about the structure of language. New, language-relevant rules could be added to the machine and, if the new rules didn't interact unfavorably with the old in some unanticipated way, the computer might actually be able to diagnose both diseases and the English language, but the machine still would have no knowledge of how to learn about physics or car mechanics or art, ad infinitum.

This limitation is the same that is encountered when people expect simple machine horsepower to provide the solution to AI problems. If the proper breadth of knowledge isn't already part of the computer's foundation, no amount of speedup can produce the correct results. Likewise, without a wide range of background information and rules to relate that information, no learning system can hope to go beyond the confines of the areas of its expertise. There are multiple dimensions of knowledge in existence, and a two-dimensional machine will never learn or generate knowledge about the multidimensional world.

Knowledge of the Self

Unlike these future computers, people are considered to be universal in the sense that they can conceivably learn about anything. Just as with computers, the learning process can be made simpler if we have someone to instruct us about the relevant information and to impart rules specific to dealing with the handling of this information. Even without such assistance, however, people can learn about areas in which they've had no previous direct exposure. We've developed, or innately have, learning mechanisms that serve us well throughout our multidimensional world.

One area in which even people struggle is the act of introspection. How did I learn this new information? How am I able to understand and respond to another speaker? Why do I get confused when confronted with too many facts in too short a time? Questions like these are difficult for people to answer, a fact that points to an intriguing observation: Perhaps our own system of thought is "self" limited in the sense that it's very hard to describe the self. In fact, it's this difficulty in analyzing our own thought processes that makes it so tough to program machines to mimic these activities. Even when we develop computers that give the same results as humans, we can't be certain that the machines use anywhere near the methods that people use to work on the problems.

The intriguing aspect of this is that maybe, given the self-limitations of our thought processes, a more complete system of thinking can be devised. Modifying basic human processes is no easy task, but computers offer us an ideal testing ground to explore different, and possibly more powerful, methods of thinking. Someday computers may not only say, "I think, therefore I am," but will go beyond this and say, "Here is how I think."

The Curiosity to Know

In the end, it's the insights that artificial intelligence provides into the workings of our own minds that ensures its continued role. Despite the concerns some hold about the prospect of thinking machines, artificial intelligence will proliferate because people are constantly striving to learn more about themselves and about their world. AI holds forth not only the guarantee of better dissemination of information already known, but also the promise of generating knowledge so far undiscovered. This promise is too great a lure to ignore or to arbitrarily restrict the technology, and it's foolish to think the AI genie will ever be placed back in its bottle. It's important to remember, however, that many of the promises made by AI are still a long way off.

We can begin to see the realization of some of this potential in the AI products that are just now taking their first steps into our lives. These products suggest a future scenario in which people and computers will work in tightly coupled systems. The people will fulfill the role of providing the genius and the direction, the computer will serve as a very intelligent tool that attempts to thoroughly prove all the various assertions or questions put to it. On occasion, the machine may even come up with some fresh insights of its own.

The latter scenario won't be feasible for many years, but should it occur, will it really be so frightening? Probably not. By the time of such machines, we will have grown more familiar with computers and more certain of their strengths and weaknesses. In the end it will be up to us how we exploit those characteristics, not up to the machines. We're just now beginning this journey, and it promises to be a fascinating one.

Index

A

Advanced Micro Devices, 137
Aggregates, 58–60
Allied (co.), 137
Alvey, 111–112
Ambiguity, 49–50, 57–58
Apple Computer, 146, 148
ART, 30, 36
ATN. *See* Augmented transition
    network
Augmented transition network
    (ATN), 43, 44–51, 79

B

Babbage, Charles, 6
BART (Bay Area Rapid Transit),
    105–106
BASIC, 27, 168
Bell Laboratories, 9
Bin picking, 170
BMC Industries, 137
Box-Jenkins Analysis, 62

C

C, 27, 35, 36, 95
CADACEUS, 106
CAI. *See* Computer-assisted instruction
Chomsky, Noam, 42, 49
COBOL, 27, 29

Computer Professionals for Social
    Responsibility (CPSR), 107
Computer-assisted instruction (CAI),
    167–168
Computers
  binary system, 22–23
  ENIAC, 6
  history, 6–8
  personal, 160–161
  processing levels, 19–23
  PSI, 116
  specialized artificial intelligence,
    34–36
  user interaction, 13–14
  See also Hardware; Software
Congressional Office of Technology
    Assessment, 133
Control Data Corp., 115, 137
Cray, 115
Custom development, 96–98

D

DARPA. *See* Defense Advanced
    Research Projects Agency
Dartmouth College, 9, 167–168
Data
  analysis by natural language
    processing, 62–63
  conceptual view of, 55–57

Data *(continued)*
  logical view of, 55–56
  physical view of, 55–56
  See also Databases
Databases
  aggregates, 58–60
  vs. knowledge bases, 72–77, 117
  summarization, 60–62
Dataflow, 115–116
Data General, 148, 162
Decision trees, 69–72
Defense Advanced Research Projects
    Agency (DARPA), 106, 139,
    162
  funding, 132–133
  Strategic Computing Initiative,
    132–133
Defense Department (U.S.), 12,
    106–107
Defense Advanced Research Projects
    Agency (DARPA), 106,
    132–134, 139, 162
Definition, 4–6
Dennis, Jack, 115
Digital Equipment, 97, 100, 137,
    147, 148, 162

E
Eckert, J. Presper, 6
Education, 149–151, 167–168
England. *See* Great Britain
ESP, 119
ESPRIT (European Strategic Pro-
    gram for Research and
    Development in Information
    Technology), 111
European Economic Community,
    111
Expert systems, 11, 67–68
  abstraction levels, 79–80
  decision trees, 69–72
  fact-intensive applications, 81

  inference process, 77–79
  knowledge bases, 72–77, 80–84
  product development, 93–98,
    164–165

F
Fifth-Generation Project, 11–12,
    111
  approach, 120–122, 131–132
  companies involved, 112–113
  difficulties, 120–127
  inferencing, 113–114
  knowledge bases, 117
  language selection, 117–121
  parallel processing, 114–117
  U.S. effort compared, 131–137
FOCUS, 28
FORTRAN, 27, 29
Fuchi, Kazuhiro, 112, 113, 118, 119
Fujitsu Ltd., 113

G
General Motors, 104
Generic applications, 95–96
Great Britain, 112–113, 126

H
Hardware
  evolution, 6–7, 19–21
  inferencing, 114
  toolkit market, 100
Harris (co.), 137
Heuristics, 8
Hewlett-Packard, 100, 147, 148
History, 6–13
Hitachi Ltd., 113
Honeywell, 137
Human intelligence. *See* Intelligence,
    human

I
IBM, 9, 36, 100, 125, 132, 138

IBM *(continued)*
    product development, 146–147,
        162
ICOT. *See* Institute for New
    Generation Computer Technology
Image processing, 117, 170
Inference mechanism, 80–81
    backward chaining, 77–78
    forward chaining, 78
Inferencing, 22, 113–114
Inman, Admiral Bobby, 138–139,
    142
Institute for New Generation
    Computer Technology (ICOT),
        112, 116, 117, 118, 119,
        120–121, 124, 132
Intel, 148
Intellect, 33, 89, 136, 165–166
Intellicorp, 162
Intelligence, human, 17–19

J
Japan
    economic history, 122–124
    Fifth-Generation Project, 11–12,
        111, 112–127, 131–137
    Ministry of International Trade
        and Industry, 133–134
Job threat, 104

K
KEE, 30, 36
KLO, 119
Knowledge bases
    vs. databases, 72–77, 117
    inference mechanism, 77–81
    problem selection, 82–84
    querying, 76–77
Knowledge processing, 8

L
Language. *See* Natural language

processing; Programming
    languages; Speech technology
Large-scale integration (LSI), 6–7,
    22
Lexicon, 57, 58
LISP, 34–36, 95
    computers, 35–36
    vs. PROLOG, 117–122
Logical Inferences Per Second
    (LIPS), 114
Lovelace, Ada, 6

M
Marcus, Mitch, 49
Market, 10–13
Martin Marietta Aerospace, 137
Massachusetts Institute of Technol-
    ogy. *See* MIT
Matsushita Electric Industry Co.,
    Ltd., 113
Mauchly, John, 6
MCC. *See* Microelectronics and
    Computer Technology Corp.
McCarthy, John, 9
Microelectronics and Computer
    Technology Corp. (MCC)
    funding, 138–139
    membership, 137–138
    prospects, 140–142
    staffing, 139–140
Military systems. *See* Defense
    Department
Minsky, Marvin, 9, 67–68
MIT (Massachusetts Institute of
    Technology), 9, 49, 67, 115
MITS, 146
Mitsubishi Electronic Corp., 113,
    116
Mostek (co.), 137
Motorola, 138
MSA, 101
Moscow Academy of Sciences, 113

Multiple linear regression, 62
Multiprocessors. *See* Parallel processing
Musashino Laboratories, 113

N
National Semiconductor, 138
Natural language processing, 10
   aggregates, 58–60
   ambiguity, 49–50, 57–58
   data-analysis capability, 62–63
   data, interaction with, 55–58
   history, 41–43
   Intellect, 33, 89, 136, 165–166
   pragmatics, 52–53
   product development, 89, 166
   semantic primitives, 53–54
   semantics, 50–51
   speech recognition, 63–64
   summarization, 60–62
   syntax, 43–50
NCR, 138
NEC Corp., 113
NOMAD, 28
Norris, William C., 137

O
OKI Electric Industry Co., Ltd., 113

P
Parallel processing, 22, 114–116,
   126, 134–136
Parse tree, 46–50, 51
   ATN, 48, 79
   wait and see, 49
Parsing. *See* Parse tree
Pascal, 27
Personal computers, 160–161
PL/1, 27, 35
Pragmatics, 52–53
Product development, 87–89, 162,
   175–186
   business' role, 102–103

difficulties, 89–93, 97–98, 100
entrepreneurial,142–149
expert systems, 93–98, 164–165
IBM, 146–147, 162
levels, 95–96
MCC, 140–142
minicomputer, 148
types, 96–102
unnecessary, 158–160
Programming languages, 23–30
   assembly language, 26
   definition, 25
   education, 150–151
   evolution, 23–30
   fifth-generation, 98–100
   implementation languages, 95
   machine language, 25–26
   nonprocedural languages, 28
   procedural languages, 27
   rule-based programming, 28–29,
      30–34
   translations, 27, 29
   See also specific languages
PROLOG, 34–36, 95
   vs. LISP, 117–122
Public acceptance, 103–108

R
RAMIS, 28
RCA, 138
Robinson, J. Alan, 118, 119
Robotics, 68, 103–104, 170
Rochester, Nathaniel, 9
Rockwell (co.), 138
Rule-based programming, 28–29,
   30–34, 82
   debugging aids,33–34
   languages, 30. *See also specific*
      languages

S
S.1, 30, 36

Schank, Roger, 49
SCI. *See* Strategic Computing
    Initiative
Semantics, 50–51
Shannon, Claude, 9
Sharp Corp., 113
SIMPOS, 119
Software
  evolution, 7
  role in artificial intelligence, 7–8
  vertical applications, 101–102
Speech technology, 63–64, 117,
    169–170
  meaningful sentences, 64
  meaningless sentences, 64
  single word applications, 64
Sperry (co.), 138
Strategic Computing Initiative (SCI)
  Fifth-Generation Project com-
    pared, 131–137
Summarization, 60–62
Syntax
  ambiguity, 49–50
  augmented transition network
    (ATN), 43, 44–51
  context-free, 43–44
  See also Parse tree
Syntelligence, 162
Syracuse University, 118, 119

T
Teknowledge, 162
Texas Instruments, 100, 162

Toolkits, knowledge-engineering,
    98–101, 163–164
  hardware vendors, 100
  problem types, 99
Toshiba Corp., 113
Translators, machine, 9

U
Union of Soviet Socialist Republics.
    See USSR
University of Pennsylvania, 6
University of Tokyo, 112
USSR, 113

V
Vertical applications, 101–102
Very-large-scale integration (VLSI),
    22, 23
Vision, machine, 170
Voice-activated typewriters, 64
Voice technology. *See* Speech
    technology

W
Weapons. *See* Defense Department

X
XCON, 97, 135
Xerox, 140

Y
Yale University, 49

ABOUT THE AUTHORS

Larry R. Harris received his Ph.D. in Computer Science from Cornell University. Dr. Harris is author of *Intellect*—the first successful commercially available natural language processing system—and a founder and president of Artificial Intelligence Corporation. He is an international authority on natural language analysis and database systems, having lectured throughout North America, and in Europe, Japan, Australia, Brazil, and the U.S.S.R. He was also Professor of Computer Science at Dartmouth College and Visiting Professor at the Laboratory of Artificial Intelligence at the Massachusetts Institute of Technology.

Dwight B. Davis has covered the computer field as a Senior Editor with *High Technology* magazine for three years. In this capacity, he has written feature articles about topics including natural language processing, supercomputers, and the Defense Department's Strategic Computing Initiative. Prior to his current position, he spent six years in the computer trade press. He holds a Master's degree in Science Journalism from Boston University.

Larry R. Harris   Dwight B. Davis